A Special Heart

A Special Heart

An Amazing Journey of Hope, Love, and Courage in Raising a Special Child to Reach His Full Potential

JUDY ZIMLICHMAN

A SPECIAL HEART
An Amazing Journey of Hope, Love, and Courage in Raising a Special Child to Reach His Full Potential

iUniverse books may be ordered through booksellers or by contacting:

iUniverse
1663 Liberty Drive
Bloomington, IN 47403
www.iuniverse.com
1-800-Authors (1-800-288-4677)

Because of the dynamic nature of the Internet, any web addresses or links contained in this book may have changed since publication and may no longer be valid. The views expressed in this work are solely those of the author and do not necessarily reflect the views of the publisher, and the publisher hereby disclaims any responsibility for them.

Any people depicted in stock imagery provided by Thinkstock are models, and such images are being used for illustrative purposes only. Certain stock imagery © Thinkstock.

ISBN: 978-1-4917-9446-3 (sc)
ISBN: 978-1-4917-9447-0 (e)

Library of Congress Control Number: 2016906245

Print information available on the last page.

iUniverse rev. date: 09/20/2016

CONTENTS

ACKNOWLEDGMENTS

I would like to thank my husband and my entire family, who contributed to this book with their anecdotes and stories. Without their input, it could not have been possible.

My deepest appreciation goes to the efforts of many professionals who helped Chaim throughout the years. They were my guides and support throughout the difficult times.

Special thanks to the people in the community who are sensitive to Chaim and encourage his participation in davening and *shiurim*. An *alliyah* on Shabbat and a song at *shalosh seudos* are just some of the ways that make him feel like a valued member of the community.

We express our appreciation to everyone who calls Chaim or greets him with a smile and a kind word. It really touches his soul and makes him very happy! Thanks to the very special people in the community who have been welcoming Chaim into their homes, even when he arrives uninvited on Shabbos. These spontaneous visits make him feel very loved and very much a part of the community.

Last but not least, thanks to Chaim for being the very special person he is. It is a privilege that Hashem chose us to be his parents. He has taught us so much about life and about the human being's unlimited capacity for empathy; Chaim made us open our eyes and witness firsthand all his accomplishments, everything that so many professionals told us was absolutely impossible!

Most of all, Chaim has taught us the healing power of faith, love, laughter, and music.

Foremost, my gratitude is offered to Hashem (God) for making this book a reality.

—Judy Zimlichman and family

INTRODUCTION

The purpose for our writing this book is to share with other families, communities, and professionals our journey with Chaim. It is of great importance for us to have hope and to give our children with special needs the greatest opportunities possible. Their integration into the lives of their families and communities is essential so that they can reach their maximum potential and feel a sense of belonging.

At the time Chaim was born in 1976, the stigma of having a child with a handicap was very strong. Few services were available to families with handicapped children. Many parents who had babies with special needs placed their children into institutions or into foster care, fearful of how the rest of their families would be impacted.

These circumstances have gradually changed in recent years. Presently, in any school one can see a child in a wheelchair or with Down syndrome, a child with hearing aids, or children with a variety of special needs.

As a result of these children living with their families nowadays, the community is compelled to accept them and to develop appropriate special education programs for them. They have created social programs as well to help these children integrate successfully into *frum* community life.

In this book, I have tried to give the reader a sense of what it was like over the past forty years to parent a child who is intellectually and physically handicapped. I have also tried to show how parents can be effective advocates for their children. My family and most of the people in my community accepted Chaim and welcomed him in spite of his special needs. While watching Chaim grow up, people who met him and interacted with him became more sensitive to other children with special needs. The experiences of the past forty years are proof that if we believe in possibilities with all our hearts and souls, they can become realities. We must never give up, because Hashem helps everyone through his or her challenges.

The journey of the past forty years has been inspiring and humbling. We have tried very hard to ensure that Chaim receives the best possible care, love, education, and support. This, in turn, ensured him a good quality of life.

The Birth of Our Special Baby— the Early Years

After getting married and emigrating from Hungary in October 1971, I started a new life in Montreal, Quebec, Canada. By 1975 we were blessed with two daughters, a four-year-old and a three-year-old. After a difficult pregnancy, our son, Chaim, was born on May 8, 1976.

The obstetrician dismissed my complaints of terrible headaches and spotting during the pregnancy, which concerned me. This pregnancy somehow felt very different from my previous two. The doctor induced my labor two weeks after my due date, a labor that lasted twelve very long hours. Chaim was born malnourished and with some breathing difficulties. During the delivery he seemed to have been stuck in the birth canal and may have been deprived of oxygen. After his birth, he was taken to the neonatal intensive care unit (NICU). He was given intravenous antibiotics and put in an oxygen tent to help his breathing.

I remember waking up in my room a few hours after the delivery, but the baby was not in my room. When I asked the nurse where my baby was, she said she did not know for sure. I had a rush of adrenaline, got into a wheelchair, and wheeled myself into the nursery, but they said my baby was not there. My heart was pounding, and I felt something was very wrong. Then I went to the neonatal intensive care unit, where I found my baby. He looked scary.

He had an IV attached to his head, and he looked very scrawny. I couldn't speak; I just sat there and cried. The doctor was not sure what was wrong with my baby, but he said that Chaim needed antibiotics and some oxygen.

I couldn't believe how skinny my baby was, even though his stomach was bloated. His sucking reflex was very poor. He could not nurse, and feeding him even from a bottle was difficult. Feedings took a very long time because of his poor sucking reflex. He would drink very little, get tired, and fall asleep again. During his hospital stay, the doctors were not able to identify the cause of Chaim's difficulties.

1976—(Chaim's Birth) First-Person Notes

The bright lights are blinding my eyes. For a second I am not sure where I am. Then reality hits me, and I come to the realization that I gave birth to my baby a few hours ago. My voice mirrors my fear— "Where is my baby? He should be in my room. Where did they take him?" No one is there to answer my questions. I realize it is about two o'clock in the morning Sunday. I get out of my bed, against the advice of the nurse—who is nowhere to be found now—and find a wheelchair. Feeling safer in a seated position, I wheel myself to the nursery, but I am told my baby is not there. "So where is my baby?" I ask. They tell me to look in the intensive care unit for newborns.

I enter a new world. Tiny little bodies are wrapped up within tiny little incubators, and they are attached to many tiny tubes.

Everything in that world is tiny and fragile, existing by the grace of God. I am having a hard time breathing, and I am too scared to ask which one is my baby. At last, a nurse sees that I am about to pass out, and she looks at my bracelet to find out my identity. She wheels me to the incubator where my baby is lying still. It is hard to describe my first impression of the baby. He is asleep. His head is swollen on one side where the intravenous line is inserted to provide hydration and antibiotics for him. His skin seems dry, and his bones are visible everywhere. On the other hand, his stomach is bloated, even though, according to the doctors, he is malnourished. He reminds me of the children of Africa who are starving. All I can do is sit and cry— and cry some more …

Today my baby is two days old. I spoke to the doctors about his progress. They said that he is stable; however, he still needs some oxygen and antibiotics. It seems he was born after forty-three weeks of gestation, which caused the malnutrition and also the complications during the birth. A healthy, normal child is born after a maximum forty weeks of pregnancy. The doctor says, "I am not sure if he is going to make it." He is talking without any emotions. It shocks me how detached he seems. I wonder if he is able to imagine what a mother may feel at that moment. Does he realize that I feel he may be giving a death sentence to my baby? I cannot fathom what ramifications his words have for our future. I can only try to think and ask the doctors, "What can I do right now to help my baby survive?"

After twelve days in the NICU, he was discharged from the hospital. The bris (circumcision) took place when he was fourteen days old. For a healthy baby boy, the bris is done on the eighth day after his birth.

It took two whole months for Chaim to regain the weight he lost during the first three weeks of his life. He was a quiet and passive baby who ate every two hours for two and a half years. He had difficulty with his digestion. He vomited frequently and then had to be fed again. This was the only way for us to prevent him from losing weight. In the beginning I could not imagine how I could do this around the clock and also take care of the rest of the family's needs. However, I later learned to go on with little sleep, for about three years. There were times when I would just sit down and cry from exhaustion, and I asked Hashem to please help me go on.

When people heard that we had a new baby, and he was not well, their mazel tov was strained and quiet. They felt uncomfortable asking about the baby's difficulties. The above attitude made me wonder if the birth of a handicapped baby was seen by people as a blessing or a tragedy. People said some hurtful things: "God must be punishing you for something you have done"; "There must be something wrong with your family's genes." Another person said, "God gave you a precious gift to nurture and love. You should feel honored that you were chosen to be the parents of such a pure soul." At that time I was not sure how I felt, except that I needed to focus on one day at a time.

It was physically exhausting to provide Chaim with the constant care he needed and mentally draining to continuously worry about his health. He was hospitalized frequently with various infections and very high fevers. There were times when he needed to be in the hospital for a week or two. I never left him alone. One time the doctors were unable to get his fever under control. Chaim did not want to drink, and he was barely moving. We were worried about complications such as meningitis, because of high fever and dehydration. The doctors told us just to leave him alone and "let nature take its course." No one could give us reassurance that our son would survive!

As I sat by his bedside and said *tehillim* around the clock, I hoped that he would gradually improve. Watching his labored breathing was pure torture. I could not imagine letting a life slip away without even trying to do something for him. I cried and slept for a few minutes. Then I would wake suddenly and touch his body to make sure that he was still breathing. I continued this heartbreaking vigil for many more days.

Finally we could not just stand by any longer without doing anything. So we asked for guidance from the *toshe* rebbe, Rabbi Meshulam Lowy, who told us to try to feed him watermelon juice with a medicine dropper—one drop every minute and then increase it very slowly.

Miraculously, Friday evening he did open his mouth and was willing to swallow the drop of juice. By midnight his fever started to go down; within a day, he was fine and was allowed to go home.

Thus continued the fervent hope for small miracles, frequent visits to doctors, and our constant vigilance to Chaim's health.

These times were very trying because of Chaim's increasing care needs, while at the same time struggling to meet the needs of the rest of the family. Staying up through the night and caring for Chaim during the day felt like an endless task. My own family lived overseas, so they could not help me. My husband's family worked very long hours in their restaurant, so they were not able to help me either. My husband also worked long hours.

When Chaim needed to be hospitalized, I stayed with him there around the clock. My husband was left on his own to make arrangements for our two other small children and also to manage things at home. Once Chaim came home from the hospital, I was left on my own to take care of the children and the house. I felt that Hashem helped me every moment to make it through each day.

By the time Chaim was eighteen months old, we realized he was not developing normally. He was not yet walking, and he showed signs of fine and gross motor difficulties. We took him to a specialist to have a developmental evaluation. He was diagnosed with Williams syndrome (WS), which is recognized as a combination of physical and intellectual characteristics these children have.

The accompanying health concerns can range from mild to severe, such as heart problems, hypercalcaemia, poor mouth control, poor gross and fine motor coordination, "lazy eyes," hypercaustic problems, and social communication difficulties.

We thanked Hashem that Chaim had a mild form of WS, which meant more hope for his development.

It took six months to get an appointment with a specialist who was familiar with WS. He confirmed the diagnosis and told us our son would always be a "vegetable." He suggested we place him in an institution and forget about him and have other children. Hearing his words made us feel like he was giving up on our son. It felt as if lightning had hit us! This child did not even have a chance to get help from therapists yet, and they were already condemning him as "hopeless"?

Following Chaim's diagnosis, I spent hours in medical libraries researching information about Williams syndrome. At that time the research identified only twenty-seven children in North America with this syndrome. Because English is not my mother tongue, it was that much more of a challenge to become familiar with the language used in the medical books and journals. This was also very time consuming. However, it was important to me. So I hired a babysitter once a week, to allow myself the free time. Starting around this time in my life, I developed a new coping skill in difficult situations: the more information I learned about the relevant subject, the more I felt I could understand it and maybe find some solutions. This approach also gave some sense of control at a time when my whole life seemed to have turned upside down.

My thoughts were focusing on the questions of how to parent a child with special needs and how to nurture my other two small children. It was difficult to meet Chaim's seemingly endless needs. His survival had to be my priority.

My husband felt that Chaim would grow out of whatever "the problem" was. He was in denial, disbelief, and shock. He could not fathom that this child would remain handicapped forever. He had little contact with Chaim because he did not understand how to relate to him. Chaim could not understand much at that time, and he needed constant care. By the time my husband returned home from work, the children were in bed. He spent time with the children mainly on the weekends.

There was a sense of embarrassment in some family members that a handicapped child was born into the family. Some thought it was a punishment from Hashem for some sin committed! This nearly tore my heart out. It took all my effort just to make it through each day. When I took Chaim to shul, some of the children made fun of him, which made him feel very sad. Adults stared at him or ignored him. This was heartbreaking for us to witness. However, during those years, children and adults were not exposed to or used to seeing handicapped children within the community. They did not understand what they were seeing and were worried that it may be contagious. The community was not sensitized to the needs of special children, and during those years, integration was not a common idea in our society.

When my friends and their children saw Chaim on the street or in the park and realized that he looked different, they were uncomfortable and did not know what to say. This hurt me very much. It was very isolating not to be able to share my daily challenges and struggles with anyone who could understand.

There were no support groups or networking opportunities for parents with special-needs children at that time. It took me a long time to be able to bring up the subject and talk openly with my friends about Chaim's difficulties.

During these challenging times, when Chaim was two and a half years old, we had a new baby girl. She was a very easygoing and happy baby. She gave us much happiness and also provided us with more strength to deal with the daily challenges of Chaim's needs. Our two other daughters were very excited about the new baby in our family.

It was a different experience for them this time; they were older, and this new baby was healthy, more responsive, interactive, and a lot of fun. They were able to play with her, and she smiled every time they picked her up from her crib. I was also much more relaxed following the new baby's birth, seeing that she was healthy.

The positive aspects of our journey with Chaim were the tremendous emotional, intellectual, and spiritual growth we all experienced through living with Chaim and through our constant seeking and searching for solutions. We were committed to give Chaim the best possible quality of life and a chance to enable him to achieve his maximum potential. The contact I made with the many professionals was helpful in providing me with more information, support, and resources.

We took Chaim to see a genetic specialist at a hospital out of town when he was two to three years old. The doctor spent a lot of time predicting future problems, even though she had not seen any children with Williams syndrome over the age of thirteen. She predicted that he would never be able to take care of himself physically and that he would not be able to talk, walk, or have a normal life. This was one more of those times when it took all our strength just to go on and have hope for Chaim's future.

In my search for more answers, I took Chaim to New York to see a cardiologist. Chaim had a heart murmur, which I felt may have been affecting his development at that time. They did many very painful and invasive tests. Chaim became very wary of doctors and medical procedures from that time on.

Witnessing this was difficult for me. I did not tell his heart doctor in Montreal that we consulted with another cardiologist. The New York doctor agreed with the diagnosis and treatment plan of the cardiologist in Montreal.

To my surprise, at my next appointment with the Montreal cardiologist, he told me he played golf frequently with the doctor I saw in New York. He also told me that they discussed Chaim's situation! I was very embarrassed. But it made me realize there is no purpose in running to out-of-town doctors, because Montreal had excellent pediatric specialists.

My challenge was to accept what was not changeable and move on with helping Chaim with what was available: physical and occupational therapy, socialization, nutrition, and special education.

A few months later, I met an exceptional doctor at the emergency room of a children's hospital. This was one of our many visits with Chaim because of his fevers and infections. Chaim was very frightened of doctors in white lab coats. The minute he saw one, he was already weeping. When this doctor arrived to examine Chaim, he was wearing no white lab coat, and he pulled out a puppet from his pocket and started playing with Chaim. They became instant friends, which lasted for many years. This doctor continued following Chaim, monitored his progress every few years, and gave me useful guidance based on his observations. He was very helpful and had a good understanding of Chaim's abilities and disabilities.

Everything he said remains true today. He explained that children like Chaim may learn things on a more superficial level, but they are unable to develop an in-depth logical understanding of a subject. He gave us hope and support and pointed us in the right direction, helping us to connect to the therapeutic programs that would benefit Chaim.

From a very young age, Chaim attended various specialized therapeutic programs to help improve his skills. His fine motor skills were poor. This affected his hands and his ability to draw and cut. One of his occupational therapists spent eight to nine months working with Chaim, to help him learn the fine motor skills required to draw a circle or cut with scissors.

The first time I noticed that Chaim mastered holding and using a pair of scissors was when I saw him cutting our living room curtain into shreds! Of course I was delighted that he finally was able to get the hang of using scissors, but my curtain was ruined. Talk about mixed feelings!

His gross motor development was delayed as well, which affected his walking. It also took a long time for Chaim to adapt to heights, and with the help of the physical therapist, he learned to walk up and down the stairs.

Chaim attended a regular Jewish preschool, but as he was getting older, the gap between his functioning and the other children's was getting wider. One of the high school boys told us a few weeks after school started that Chaim used to roll down the stairs when he went to nursery school, because he was either unable or afraid to go down the stairs in the usual manner. This young man realized the problem and used to wait for Chaim every morning when he arrived at school, so he could help Chaim go down the stairs.

Chaim had difficulty keeping up with nearly all aspects of school, and by kindergarten age it was clear that he would need a special education program. When Chaim was very frustrated by demands made of him that he could not do, he used to hit his own face. This was very frightening to watch! He would also cry when someone raised their voice, and he would stare openmouthed at people he did not know or was frightened of. These behaviors were also obstacles for him in making friends.

The staff at Chaim's preschool called us to say that they were not able to accommodate Chaim's educational needs within the current framework of the school. The teachers in the regular preschool classes did not know how to work with Chaim; neither did they understand his abilities or his disabilities.

Removing Chaim from the Jewish school was not an option for us. His right to be educated in a Jewish school—just like his siblings and all the other Jewish children in our community—had to be protected. We arranged a short-term compromise with the school: Chaim would go two days a week to a special (non-Jewish) therapeutic program, and the other days he would attend the Jewish school. They accepted this as an interim solution.

When a child's abilities and disabilities fluctuate greatly in different areas, it is more challenging to provide an education for him. That has been the situation for the professionals who worked with Chaim throughout the years. On some levels he is able to function fairly well; he is independent physically but requires close supervision and guidance. He speaks several languages but has difficulty with basic reading, writing, and counting. When we asked a specialist why Chaim was not yet reading at the age of eight, he answered that all effort was being made to teach him, but there was no guarantee that he would learn how to read. We could only hope and pray.

He mastered reading and writing at a second-grade level.

Another weak point for Chaim is judgment. His ability fluctuates, and because of this, people have difficulty understanding what is "really wrong with him."

Many professionals have closely followed Chaim's development, education, and progress, constantly monitoring his strengths and weaknesses over the years. This allowed his teachers and therapists to readjust the focus of their work on a regular basis. Chaim was making slow progress while learning all day in the resource room. He was integrated into a regular class for a little period of time each day and also spent recess with the children from the regular classes.

Chaim had a good relationship with the other children in the special education class. He was sensitive, protective, and helpful to the children who were lower functioning than he.

The special education teachers were very dedicated to each child's needs. Their aim was for every child to reach his potential.

However, Chaim was often sad because he did not have friends. Very few children from the regular class wanted to play with him during recess or at his house. When I did arrange for a classmate to come and play with Chaim at home, Chaim did not know how to interact with a "normal" child on his level. The child did not want to come back anymore. Chaim does not see himself as physically different from others, and he is not. He was always trying to identify himself with the "normal" children and not with other handicapped children. This caused him much frustration throughout the years.

JASE Establishes Jewish Special Education Classes in Montreal

*B*efore 1981, in the Montreal Jewish day schools, there were no special education programs for children. They attended special public schools, and they did not receive any Jewish education to which their siblings were entitled.

The year 1980 brought the beginning of my meetings and networking with community leaders about the need to start a special education program within our community. At first there were doubts whether there was a real need. Then it was clear that there were enough children to start two classes. There was no funding available from the government or the organized Jewish community. This was a tremendously challenging situation! I started working day and night to try to establish a new organization for Jewish special education in Montreal.

The goal was to start new programs within the Jewish day school system for the children who required and were entitled to a Jewish special education. It is hard to look back at those years and understand the amount of energy it took to develop and establish new special education programs in the community.

In May 1980, I was introduced to a generous philanthropist from our community. He agreed to establish and spearhead a newly formed association called Jewish Association for Special Education (Degel Naftali) JASE. He assembled a board of directors and started raising the necessary funds to start two special education classes in September 1981. We worked constantly to secure the income needed for our program. We organized fundraising events such as auctions, tea parties, concerts, and mailings, which brought in the necessary funds to finance our program.

Starting to work as the executive director of this new association in 1980 opened up a whole new world for me. The newly established organization was founded to manage the activities of the special education programs.

We needed to organize meetings and work with the lay leadership and professionals. I had to be up to date on information about special education and government regulations, so I would feel confident when making presentations to the government and industry professionals. I was learning on the job and developing a new project that had never been done before in the Jewish community.

The principal of a special school was instrumental in helping our organization set up the educational structure for our resource rooms. She also arranged for the psychoeducational evaluation for each of our students.

Her staff was available to us for consultation, and she remained involved and very helpful to us throughout the years. Her tremendous understanding and sensitivity to the unique cultural and religious needs of the children of our community was heartwarming and very much appreciated.

To keep our expenses to a minimum, the office of the organization was located in my house for several years, rent-free. I worked as a volunteer executive director for the first five years, until we were successful in our negotiations with the government for financial support.

It was quite surprising that the parents whose children needed a special program were initially very hesitant to enroll them in the special education classes. They were very worried about the stigma of sending a child to a resource room. These children had various needs. Some were intellectually and/or physically handicapped, some had vision or hearing impairments, while others had learning disabilities. Each child was to be integrated into a regular class for some time during the school day. They all spent recess and nonacademic activities with their respective classes.

The special classes started on September 1, 1981, in two mainstream Jewish day schools, with twelve students. With the input of our consultants, we hired teachers, evaluated the children, and met with the parents. After we bought materials and supplies, we were ready to start the school year. For the first five years, I coordinated all educational, administrative, and fundraising programs.

By 1985, our student body has grown to forty-two. Seeing the children succeed in the special education JASE classes gave me tremendous joy and satisfaction. It felt like a dream come true. The children were taught on a one-on-one basis. Therefore we had thirty-two part-time teachers on our staff. As the program grew, we hired two coordinators to supervise the teachers and the educational programs.

It was a constant challenge to coordinate the different aspects of the program within the host schools. There were some children who transferred to these schools from another school specifically because they needed a special education program.

Although our association was an independent organization within the schools, the children were accepted and embraced by the host schools. JASE was seen as providing an invaluable service to all the children.

JASE's work included extensive public education and sensitization of the community about special education, learning disabilities, and special needs. At the time, all this effort felt like climbing Mount Everest.

I was constantly pushing the boundaries of all systems— educational, social, and communal. However, my attitude was that nothing was impossible; it just takes effort, time, patience, and lots of prayer.

Our association organized workshops and public-education programs to sensitize the community and the schools about the needs of the special children. As a result of our organization's work with the community and the provincial government, and after several years of negotiating, we started receiving financial support from the government. They gradually increased the number of children eligible for the funds that paid for the special education they needed. In later years, several other Jewish day schools also started receiving money to provide special education programs for their children.

As a result of our unrelenting negotiation with the government, the Jewish community day schools received

a gradual increase in government grants for the special-needs students.

Because of our special education program's superior quality, it became a model for other schools that wanted to serve and integrate children with special needs.

The expressions of gratitude from the parents whose children were finally receiving the special teaching they desperately needed was the greatest reward for those of us involved in the organization.

Summer Camps and the Yachad Trips

*I*n the summers, Chaim attended overnight camps after the age of eight. This was the first time he was away from home. He needed social interaction with other children, and the rest of the family needed some respite for the first time since Chaim was born. It also allowed me to spend more one-on-one time with the other children without worrying about Chaim.

At camp, Chaim had his own special counselor (shadow) with him, who was very attentive and accompanied Chaim to all the activities. Chaim enjoyed the social life in camp. However, he had a hard time adapting to the new routine. There was concern about his safety because he was unable to fend for himself. He was in a bunk with children younger than he. During our first visit, he proudly showed us the inside of his bunk, and his belongings were neatly arranged. When I checked his clothing, I saw that it was still folded just as I had packed it before he went to camp. He told us that laundry was done once a week, but he used only a few of his clean clothes and wore the same things over and over. He thought that keeping his things neat just as they were packed would make us happy. It was hard not to laugh or cry when he said this. He didn't understand that his laundry would be done in camp and that he should wear all his clothing.

The following two summers, Chaim went to an American overnight camp for children with disabilities. He was the highest-functioning camper there, and he mainly interacted with the staff. This was typical of Chaim's social behavior. The counselors were exceptionally kind and knowledgeable about children who were handicapped. Chaim had a special job in that camp: he organized the siddurim after davening and kept the shul neat. He has many fond memories from there, one of which was of the lady cook who was very nice to him and whose food was delicious.

The following two years, Chaim was fortunate to be able to participate in trips to Israel and the East Coast of the United States with a special-needs American organization. This is an international organization that provides programs and summer trips for Jewish youths and adults with special needs.

Chaim traveled with this group to Israel in the summer of 1998. The trip provided Chaim with an unforgettable experience. He loved it, even though aspects of it were difficult for him. He is obsessive about his things being in the same place. He is also obsessive about cleanliness. When traveling, you live out of a suitcase and move from place to place. This was very hard for Chaim.

He has many fond memories of Israel. He described for us in great detail the rooms they lived in on the kibbutz. The farm animals were intriguing to Chaim. He could smell the cows from his window. He milked the cows and fed them hay. The trips to the Kotel, the streets in Jerusalem, Masada, and the Bedouin people were unforgettable to him.

He also noted the special foods he saw: fresh pretzels and roasted chestnuts, popcorn, and nuts on an outdoor woodstove.

The following year, Chaim went with the same organization on a US trip. They went to Orlando, Florida, and EPCOT Center. Again Chaim found it difficult to sleep in different places and have his bags all over the place. At the same time, he found the EPCOT Center fun and enjoyed the company of the other people. He especially connected with the staff members.

After these trips, Chaim decided he preferred to spend his two-week vacations in town. During these vacations, his private companion took him on day trips, and Chaim enjoyed the one-to-one attention he received. It also gave Chaim a chance to make his own decisions about where he wanted to go and what he wanted to do.

An Extraordinary Bar Mitzvah and the Teen Years

*W*hen Chaim was a small boy, I never in my wildest dreams thought that he would be able to have a bar mitzvah in its traditional sense. When he was about eleven years old, we started discussing with his teachers his upcoming bar mitzvah. Everyone thought that Chaim could successfully deliver a short speech and read the haftarah, and that is exactly what he did. He practiced for many months with his bar mitzvah teacher. All along he had everyone's support. The teacher tape-recorded the whole haftarah, and Chaim listened to it daily. As a result, we all knew his whole haftarah by heart and walked around the house singing it. His sisters still remember some of his haftarah.

He struggled with putting on tefillin because he had poor fine motor coordination. His occupational therapist also helped him with this task. Finally, by the time he was required to do it, he was able to.

Chaim personally invited to his bar mitzvah everybody he had met in the city. Many people who arrived uninvited told us stories of how they had been touched in some way by Chaim.

An old lady arrived at our door a day before Chaim's bar mitzvah with a gift for him. She said that Chaim waved to her each morning on his way to school as she sat by her window. She looked forward to seeing him each morning, and she just had to share in his *simcha*!

Chaim's bar mitzvah took place on May 20, 1989, on Shabbat. Chaim was not nervous at all. During the morning davening, he was called to the Torah and said everything flawlessly. It was so quiet in the shul, you could hear a pin drop. When it was over, Chaim walked into the ladies' section of the synagogue and said, "Mammy, I told you that I could do it!" I burst into tears.

Later, during the luncheon, he said his *pshetl* flawlessly in Yiddish and English, while we were all holding our breath. Again everyone was silent; you could hear every word. At the end we all burst into tears. When he looked at me puzzled, I told him these were tears of joy and happiness. There was not a dry eye in the room.

1989—(Bar Mitzvah) First-Person Notes

The room is bathed in sunlight, and the crowd is buzzing with chatter. The celebration calls for a huge luncheon with our whole community invited. The magnificent centerpieces are straight out of the décor magazines.

After the services, the people gather for lunch and to catch up with the latest news of the community. Friends share the developments in their lives as well as some jokes. Some people just float around looking for company. One man stands still as if frozen in time.

At first you only see his big blue eyes and his huge smile. He seems young. He holds his head at an awkward angle while he is staring at some stranger. He stands out in the crowd. He kindly greets everyone but seems to belong to no one. Like a butterfly, he hops from place to place, from person to person, switching with ease between the English, Yiddish, Hungarian, and Hebrew languages.

Who is this interesting person? He is unusual but interesting. He is my son, Chaim. I walk up to him and say, "Mazel tov, Chaim! You did a beautiful job reading the Torah!" He smiles and gives me a hug. Today it is the day of his bar mitzvah. After gathering himself, he says. "I am so happy that everyone came!" By the time I blink, Chaim has disappeared; he moves on to talk to other familiar people. So goes Chaim's fascination with people and social gatherings.

This is a tremendous milestone in Chaim's life. He feels very proud of himself. He feels just like every other thirteen-year-old bar mitzvah boy.

That is what he tries to aim for all the time: to be "as normal as possible." And today he feels that he accomplished just that. He is proud of himself, and we are tremendously proud of him.

I stand rooted to the place, unable to move, tears rolling down my face. The emotions feel like a roller-coaster ride at full speed. I am speechless. The hugs and kisses from family and friends feel like being carried on a cloud of love. It seems like a movie of the past thirteen years on fast-forward mode.

And then comes the outpouring of gratitude to God and to the many people who held my hand during this heartbreaking and life-affirming and joyful journey. My mind plays games with me. It flips the pictures from the view of tragedy to the view of a spiritual journey—what could have been and what actually is today. I wonder if another parent with a small child who has special needs can take some inspiration from seeing Chaim today and watching four hundred people cheering for him with tears running down their faces. And then I tell myself that it was worth all the hard work for Chaim's development and for the future of the many other children who have benefitted and will benefit from people learning to accept and love all our children just as they are, regardless of their disabilities.

At that unforgettable moment, I felt that Chaim proved to everyone that there is hope and that parents should never give up on their child. Every parent must do his best to help his child reach his highest potential. The only thing that the special children ask from us is unconditional love and acceptance. They give so much more than they take. Chaim taught us the meaning of simcha, being truly happy with what you have. His parents and siblings have become better and more sensitive people as a result of having Chaim in their lives!

The bar mitzvah milestone made me reflect on the journey throughout the previous thirteen years, and I felt that it was worth all the struggle and hard work.

Furthermore, I explained to Chaim that after his bar mitzvah, he would count as part of a minyan, which validates that he is a valued member of society.

It has been difficult to clarify our expectations of Chaim regarding his ability to understand halacha and its daily implementation. We received guidance from community leaders in this area. A number of halachic and moral concerns were discussed regarding Chaim's growing up and what our expectation of him should be on religious issues. One of our advisors had two severely handicapped children of his own, and he was able to advise us based on his personal experience.

He felt Chaim's intellectual functioning was at such a low level that he was not obligated to observe the *mitzvos* that he could not understand. "Hashem gave you a job, and do the best you can with this special *neshama*." His guidance has made us more relaxed and flexible regarding implementing halacha in Chaim's daily life.

We know not to get upset at him if he does not understand something and he is sometimes unwilling to do it. In shul Chaim would daven too loud. This would disturb others. He feels that it is his right to daven the way he wants to do it. On Shabbosim he attends several different shuls because he likes to meet all the people. Of course when he does this, it results in Chaim only catching one-third of the davening. We are learning not to admonish him about this.

Chaim's Vocational Journey

*B*ecause Chaim needed a vocationally focused program, at the age of seventeen, he had to transfer to a non-Jewish school where such programming was available. I searched every city and many countries, including Israel, for a Jewish vocational high school or yeshiva program for Chaim. But there was none.

It was a very difficult decision for us, but we had to transfer Chaim to a special public school. In the Jewish school system, he had reached his plateau and was just marking time. This move resulted in the loss of some of his social contacts in his community.

On the other hand, educationally he was doing well at his new school. The staff in the school were sensitive and familiar with the religious and cultural issues that affected Chaim. There had been other religious Jewish children attending their school throughout the years.

After he received vocational training, there were a number of supported job placements that Chaim tried throughout the years. The most memorable and longest-lasting one was at a law firm. One of the senior attorneys at the firm was the most sensitive person one could find.

Chaim used to go to work in a white shirt, vest, and tie every day, and he was very proud of himself. His work entailed organizing the mail and delivering it to the many offices.

In order to make things easier for Chaim, all the staff members in the law office wore name tags so he would be able to identify them. He loved to talk sports with the staff. One of the employees even took Chaim to a baseball game.

One of the lawyers liked Chaim very much and made him a surprise birthday party. I found out recently that the same lawyer wrote a book, and in it he wrote about Chaim and also put in a picture of Chaim and himself.

The staff of the law firm loved Chaim. He was polite, cheerful, and cooperative. However, after about two years, Chaim could not cope with the pressure of the workplace and was transferred to another worksite.

Chaim used to take the bus to work every day. The bus driver liked Chaim because Chaim said good morning and asked the driver how he was doing. One Shabbos morning Chaim was going to shul, and the bus was just passing in front of our house. The driver stopped especially for Chaim, so he could take the bus. My husband explained to the driver that on Shabbos, Chaim does not go to work and thanked the driver very kindly for his caring.

Many years ago, Chaim was trained to travel to and from work, however, he is no longer using the public-transportation system. He is very vulnerable and distractible, and we had a couple of scary incidents that made us decide to have him travel by taxi for the handicapped. Once when he traveled by Metro, there was an emergency, and the Metro passengers had to get off at a stop that was unfamiliar to him. He asked the police for help, but they ignored him.

We spent hours calling the police and the Metro. Finally, Chaim borrowed a quarter from a stranger and phoned us, but he could not tell us his location. A stranger explained to him what the area was called. Chaim is unable to deal with new situations that he is not prepared for in advance.

Chaim seemed to have reached a plateau in his physical and emotional development when he was around twenty years old. From then on, he developed anxiety, compulsiveness, behavior difficulties, and a poor attention span. All of this affected his ability to work. He was obsessed that his clothing might become dirty or wear out. On the advice of his psychiatrist, he was put on medication, which was somewhat helpful. Later he became obsessed with playing with his tzitzis, his yarmulke, or his buttons. He continued until they tore. These behaviors were not dangerous but were very annoying and impaired his ability to function. Chaim gets anxious easily, particularly when there is a change in his daily routine. *Yomim Tovim* are difficult for him because of the longer hours in shul and lots of free time on his hands.

Because of Chaim's increased need for support at work, he was transferred to a sheltered workshop for adults with special needs. These are places for people who require constant supervision in their work environment. He adjusted well to the workshop and has been working there for the past nine years. He receives minimum wage for his work, and this makes him feel "normal," just like other working people.

Chaim's Personality and His Social Life

*C*haim's personality, strengths, and weaknesses are all part of the puzzle of who he is. His abilities are amazing! He has an excellent memory, speaks several languages, and has a beautiful voice. His lack of understanding of dangerous situations and poor ability to interpret social cues continue to cause us worry. He is unable to manage money and therefore can only carry a small amount. He is vulnerable in unfamiliar public places.

He is very respectful, polite, and sensitive to everyone, regardless of age, gender, or race. He loves to help people. Whether in his group home, at the workshop, or in shul, he is always ready to help someone who seems to need support. He is extremely friendly with people he knows and also with strangers. Wherever we go, we meet people who know and greet Chaim. He has a sixth sense about people. He is able to look at the face of someone he knows and tell how the person feels. He senses an undercurrent in a person and responds with caring and friendship. Chaim loves to give advice and help others.

His parents and sisters always treated him as a normal child. His sisters love him dearly, and when they were younger, they took turns spending time with him. They were an important part of his social circle. He was not a burden for them, and they embraced him with love and compassion.

We, as parents, were concerned that he should not become a burden to his sisters. I often wondered if his sisters felt neglected because Chaim required round-the-clock care until he was three years old. He did not sleep well and was very scared of the dark. We talked to the girls about Chaim's difficulties, and I spent some time with each child alone, so they would have my undivided attention. This felt like a balancing act that I could never do perfectly.

Chaim's sisters enjoyed spending time with him. They played ball frequently, and he became an excellent ball player. When the other children did not want to include Chaim in a game, his sisters advocated for him and talked to the other kids to let Chaim have at least one turn. It was difficult for Chaim to follow the rules of the game.

Chaim would often accompany his sisters on outings with their friends, as he did not really have friends of his own to occupy his spare time.

It took one year for Chaim to master riding his two-wheeler bicycle. Chaim used to stop his bike with his shoe rather than the brake. Replacing his shoes was a small price to pay, as he could now ride on his own. Another trip to the shoe store was just a minor inconvenience in this case.

One of Chaim's favorite pastimes is to watch construction sites on the street. He is fascinated by the large machinery used in the demolition of structures. If at times we did not know where he went, we would walk down the neighborhood streets and usually find him staring at some construction site. On the other hand, Chaim was very disturbed by any loud noises, so he would cover his ears with both hands and walk around like that in noisy places.

When Chaim was younger, during the summer months we used to go to the mountains. There were other families there from our neighborhood. Any change in his environment was challenging for Chaim. New physical surroundings, new people, children, and different expectations were some of the issues we had to deal with regarding Chaim. Some of the children there did not know Chaim. They had difficulty relating to him and made fun of him. Others refused to welcome him into their games and activities because Chaim was unable to follow the rules of the game. Chaim missed his sisters as he got older—they got married and moved out of town—because they used to advocate for him and help him in difficult social situations.

After Chaim's sisters moved away, he was having a very difficult time adjusting to being the only child at home. His oldest sister got married in 1992. Chaim missed her tremendously and felt abandoned by her. He was unable to understand that she moved to Toronto because her husband worked there.

During the time when Chaim's sisters were dating, there were some people who expressed concern that there would be difficulties with *shiduchim* because of Chaim's handicap. However, Chaim's sisters felt that if anyone did not want to be a part of our family just because of Chaim, that person was not for us. The girls each wanted a husband who would feel very comfortable with Chaim and who would welcome Chaim into their future home with open arms.

In 1994, Chaim's second sister got married and also moved out of town. This was again a very difficult time of adjustment for Chaim. We made sure that he joined us for every visit to see his sisters during the following years.

Chaim was heartbroken when each of his sisters got married and left home. However, when his youngest sister—who is three years younger than he—got married, he was beside himself. He was very close to her, and also he felt that it was really his turn to get married because he is older than she.

During this sister's wedding, Chaim came into the ladies' section to dance with her, with his other sisters, and then with me. Everyone had tears in their eyes. I had no heart to tell him that it was not appropriate for him to leave the men's section and come to the ladies' side.

After all his siblings moved out, Chaim felt sad and left behind. He was also jealous that they were able to find a partner but he was not. This sense of sadness and jealousy can still be seen in Chaim when his sisters come home to visit us with their families or when we visit them. He feels incomplete when he compares himself to his siblings.

Most of Chaim's friends in the community we live in are married and have children. He meets them often in the synagogue and on the street. They are always very kind to him. However, once again he feels left behind and sad that he is not married yet. We tell him often that when the right time and the right person comes along, he may be able to get married. We try to reassure him that he is such a loving brother, son, grandson, nephew, cousin, uncle, and brother-in-law that he can still be a happy person even if he is not married.

Chaim has a limited understanding of interpersonal relationships or partnership in marriage, even though he received family-life training that included education about his sexuality. He sees it from a child's point of view. He often speaks to people about marriage and asks them to help him find a wife.

We always take Chaim with us when we go to Toronto to visit his sisters. He feels very accepted and an integral part of the extended family. His brothers-in-law are warm and caring toward him, and his nieces and nephews accept him the way he is. They have learned to respect Chaim and address him as the adult he is, despite the fact that his behavior often reflects that of a younger child.

At our family gatherings, Chaim likes to sing and give a speech. He does not need any formal preparation. He speaks well in public, and he feels valued as someone who is able to contribute to the event.

Chaim is very well liked and accepted in the shul where we daven out of town. He feels at home, and he endears himself to the people. They respond positively to his attention seeking.

While we are in Toronto, Chaim has less freedom in the community because he does not know the area and cannot walk around on his own. Therefore, he spends most of the time with family members or needs someone to accompany him when he goes out. At times, he has a *chavrusa* when we are out of town, which gives him the opportunity to develop a relationship with a new person; he enjoys learning and singing melodies.

Chaim loves to sing wherever he is. When he comes with us to visit his sisters, he goes to shul with his brothers-in-law. The people there are very welcoming to him. He sings in the middle of the shul, and the whole place sings with him. Chaim takes pride in his Jewish values and in being a productive member of his family and his community. When he attends a concert and they ask for volunteers, Chaim is the first to go on stage to sing, and he does not want to stop after one song!

He also likes to sing for the other residents and staff in his group home. He has a very good sense of humor. He loves to laugh and listen to jokes and tell jokes of his own. Badchen tapes are his favorite. Chaim loves clowning around with his nieces and nephews. He gets into fits of laughter and giggling until his tears are flowing.

Even though Chaim is able to speak several languages, his understanding of logic is limited. When his sister was expecting a baby, Chaim asked her if he was going to become an aunt or an uncle depending on the gender of the baby. He does not have a great concept of time either. The nine months of pregnancy were an unending amount of time for him. He would ask on a daily basis when the baby would be born.

Chaim has great difficulty understanding abstract concepts: how and why someone may get sick and the difference between short-term sickness and chronic illness. He often feels that a cold will last "forever" and he will "never get well." He fears illness, needles, hospitals, and death.

When the H1N1 flu affected the group home's residents, including Chaim, he was extremely agitated because everyone was wearing masks and had to stay inside the house and could not go to work. To this day, Chaim may even deny feeling sick so he does not have to stay home and be bored.

If Chaim had a bad cold and had to stay downstairs in his room because of a strong cough, he viewed this as punishment, not understanding it as a medically necessary precaution. The staff of his group home tried to calm him down and keep him occupied.

He also fears family members getting sick. He is worried that if I get sick, I will not be able to take care of his needs—buy his clothes and organize his life.

Chaim constantly seeks reassurance from people if they "really" like him, trust him, and care about him. He asks his parents never to forget him and always to take care of his needs. His compulsiveness causes him to repeat these things frequently.

As a result of Chaim's emotional struggles, his medications were increased. This helped him function better. At times, he still got into debates and heated discussions with the other workers and the staff. He does not like strict rules and the unpleasant consequences of not abiding by those rules. On the other hand, he likes to be productive and is proud of himself when he does good work. The workplace also provides him with opportunities for socialization. He is also able to go to the store near his group home by himself, where he buys snacks to take to work for the week. He enjoys having some independence, and we give him opportunities to make some of his own decisions.

Moving to a
Special Group Home

*I*n the past, if a handicapped child needed placement in a home, there were no observant Jewish homes available in our city. Some children were placed in non-Jewish homes and lost touch with their religion and cultural community.

In 1986, a group of women organized a community meeting to discuss this difficult situation and the need to establish an observant Jewish group home for multiple handicapped children. The group then implemented plans to make this dream a reality. I decided to become actively involved on the executive board because of the extreme importance of this cause. At the time, I never thought that Chaim would become a resident of a group home. Our first step was to purchase a home, getting the necessary legal documents, negotiating with the government and the social and health care agencies, so they would give us credibility and funding to open the home.

Our mission was to establish an observant group home so we could ensure that those families who were strictly observant and would not use any other facility would be able to place their children into our group home. All Jewish children are welcome to our home, as long as they and their families are able to follow the home's mandate.

After raising the funds and securing the permits, it took us some time to buy and renovate the group home. The entire building, three floors, had to be adapted to accommodate children in wheelchairs.

Finally, in 1987, the home was ready to open and receive the residents. I was very happy that we could help families who did not want to place their children in public homes but were very stressed by the day-to-day needs of caring for special children at home. Our new group home gave them a choice and a lifeline.

The group home's residents and staff are like one big family. The residents feel loved and cared for. The numerous activities within the home—like music, art, exercise, baking, birthday parties, and holiday gatherings—help the residents to develop friendships with one another and with the volunteers and neighbors. They truly feel they are part of their community. The residents go to shul, and volunteers come to the home to interact with the residents in the evenings and on weekends.

Our organization and the group homes continued to thrive and grow in 2015. We opened a second home in 2004 and are now serving many more families with residential and respite services.

The two homes are managed by one coordinator, one administrator, and a very caring and professional staff. The residents of both homes visit with one another, sharing birthday parties and holiday celebrations.

In 1997, at the age of twenty-one, Chaim felt it was time for him to move on with his life. By then, two of his sisters had married and moved out of town. He brought up the subject of moving away from home. I made the application with mixed feelings, and Chaim's name was put on a waiting list for a group home starting in 1991. Six years later, in 1997, he was admitted into the home at age twenty-one.

Chaim also talked about wanting to move away from home with some of the professionals who were working with him. In 1996, we were asked to attend a meeting with all the professionals working with Chaim. It was very intimidating for us, coming into a room where there were twelve professionals advocating for Chaim.

At that time, my husband and I did not want Chaim to leave home. The professionals made it clear to us, at a meeting in January 1994, that when Chaim turned eighteen years old—within a few months—he had the right to make his own decision. We finally agreed to let Chaim move out of the house, but we stipulated that he had to live in a fully supervised, observant Jewish home.

Our first move after the meeting with the professionals was to prepare an application for private curatorship for Chaim. Since Chaim is intellectually challenged, being his curator would allow us to make decisions for him regarding his health, living environment, and finances.

After many discussions and meetings, Chaim's move to the group home was finalized in 1997. I had mixed feelings about this move. Chaim was going to be the highest-functioning resident in the group home, and I was worried that he might copy some of the negative behaviors of the lower-functioning residents. I was also concerned about what we would do if Chaim changed his mind after a few weeks and wanted to move back home. Nevertheless, we went ahead with the move.

I missed Chaim terribly at home. Even though it was a relief not to have to supervise and occupy him every minute, I missed his laughter and chatter.

Since 1997, when he moved to the group home, Chaim has been involved in many activities that are very exciting for him: baking, Jewish programming with volunteers, horseback riding, birthday parties, bowling, and games. He enjoys the constant social interaction with the staff. He feels good about being able to help the other residents in the home who have more-complex disabilities. He likes to sing and dance for them and with them.

To maximize his quality of life, Chaim used to go with a companion to the gym on Sunday afternoons to do sports and other exercise. He enjoyed the one-on-one attention he got during these times. He also liked socializing with many people he knows from the community.

On his walk home in the neighborhood of his group home, everyone recognizes and knows Chaim. The yeshiva boys all say hello to Chaim and greet him with smiles. Chaim loves to talk to them.

We hired a private Jewish-studies teacher for Chaim when he moved to the group home. We wanted to ensure that he continued with his Jewish learning, even though he was working. The rabbi goes to Chaim's group home every day and works with him for one hour. Chaim enjoys learning and has developed a good relationship with his rebbe. He has difficulty understanding the logic of a simple halacha. This seems to be the mystery and inconsistency of his intellectual disability.

Chaim enjoys discussing on the phone all that he has learned with his brother-in-law. Each Friday Chaim shares his learning with him and expects him to reciprocate with some words of wisdom.

Chaim comes back home for every Shabbos and Yom Tov. We are very happy to have him with us, as he livens up the house with his singing, jokes, *divrei* Torahs, and by just being there. During the Friday-night meals, Chaim sings many of his favorite songs. He also shares his *dvar* Torah with us. This is a special time for all of us because he is the center of our attention. It also gives my husband and me a chance to share with him things from our lives. He enjoys sharing with us his knowledge of current world events and local politics, which he follows closely.

He likes to contribute to table conversation in a way that sometimes amazes us. He does not enjoy reading, as that is a difficult task for him. On Saturday nights Chaim returns to his group home. He asks his father to please take him "home"—meaning his group home. He loves to be with his parents at home, but he misses his friends from the group home, and he also loves his independence at the group home. We often tell him that he is privileged to have two homes where he feels very much loved and appreciated.

Chaim feels like—and is—an integral part of the family. His siblings, nieces, and nephews call him frequently. He calls us at home every morning and evening and sometimes during the day. He also calls his grandmother frequently and his aunt as well. He goes out for dinner with his aunt once a month; he looks forward to these outings very much. Chaim keeps in touch by phone with many people in the community. He is interested in knowing who is getting married, who had a baby, or who is having a bar mitzvah.

He is often invited to Shabbos lunch by community members who like him very much. There he is treated with tremendous respect and love. Chaim feels at home in their house. He enjoys talking to their children as well. Other families also invite Chaim for Shabbos lunch. Occasionally he eats with his aunt.

Part of Chaim's Shabbos routine is to attend the *shiurim* in the shuls of our neighborhood. He loves Torah and learning. He likes to sit next to the *rav* and ask relevant questions. He enjoys davening with different *minyonim*. Some of them let Chaim be the *baal tefilah*. This makes Chaim feel so happy that he talks about it for weeks.

On Shabbosim, Chaim also enjoys short visits with some of the neighborhood families with whom he feels close. He sings songs, catches up on community news, shares a dvar Torah, and hugs the babies. I used to feel embarrassed that Chaim just showed up without being invited. However, he only goes to those few families with whom he feels truly loved and accepted. These people welcome him with open arms and really enjoy his company. I am grateful to live in the small, close-knit community of Montreal, where Chaim is accepted and well-known to all.

Songs from a Special Heart— Chaim's CD

Since Chaim was a little child, he has loved music and singing. He sang before he talked. Once he heard a song, he was able to repeat it without missing a beat. He has a very good musical memory. In his twenties, many people asked him to sing a song at their simcha, and this made Chaim feel fantastic! At the shul, people ask him all the time to sing *zmiros*.

Around the age of fifteen, Chaim wanted to make a tape of his favorite songs, and I promised him that when he got older, he could do it. This was a vague promise, but the subject came up several times after that.

Finally it was time to fulfill the promise, and in October 2005, Chaim embarked on the journey of making his own CD. We met with a musician who has a recording studio in Montreal. He was very kind and patient and was willing to work with Chaim and join him on this special journey.

For me this was a tremendously satisfying and uplifting year, witnessing Chaim create his own CD, *Songs from a Special Heart.* I accompanied him and stayed in the room with him during every recording session.

There were times when he was singing in the studio that I was literally holding my breath. He was singing with his eyes closed and very focused—as if he was transported to another place and time.

==

2006—(CD) First-Person Notes

The voice brings tears to my eyes and tugs at my heart. He stands still, with eyes closed tight, hugging the microphone and oblivious to the world around him. His entire body, heart, and soul seem to be entirely entwined in his singing. His face shows total concentration. I am afraid even to breathe, so as not to disturb him or break this spell of total awe.

When he finishes the song, he looks at me and says, "I did it well, didn't I?" My only response is "Just perfect." The past minutes were unforgettable. I feel privileged to have been able to witness such pure and total joy of singing by a person. Even more so because it is my son, Chaim.

===

His face radiated pure joy! The feelings that were infused into some of his songs brought tears to my eyes. I felt that our souls were totally entwined with each other. He seemed to have surprised himself sometimes by saying, "I really did it this time, didn't I?" He knew when some extraordinary moments transpired, and that inspired him. I felt very privileged to have been there to witness those moments. It gave me a glimpse into his inner soul.

The Singing Soul and the Soaring Spirit

Chaim's CD was completed in October 2006, and people were buying it in stores. Chaim was the proudest person on earth! That was all he could talk about with everyone. He received so much acknowledgment and sincere praise from so many people that it really gave a boost to his self-esteem. His CDs were also sold in Toronto. When we visited his sisters in Toronto, Chaim would ask everyone he met if they bought his CD. On the street and in shul, people came over to Chaim and praised him about his music.

The completion of his CD was a major life accomplishment for Chaim. We know that he will always look back on it with pride. He will be able to say that he achieved something none of his siblings or friends were able to do.

Words from a Special Child's Heart

DEAR PARENTS,   Nov 19. 2010

WHOEVER HAS A HANDICAPPED CHILD, IT IS
CHALLENGING, INTERESTING, AND FUN BECAUSE WE
LEARN TO ACCEPT THEM. I HAVE WILLIAMS SYNDROME.
I LOVE MUSIC AND LEARNING, AND HELPING OUT IN THE
COMMUNITY. YOU HAVE TO HAVE PATIENCE WITH THE SPECIAL
CHILD. I HOPE YOU LEARN SOMETHING FROM MY
EXPERIENCES AND FROM MY LIFE.
SPECIAL CHILDREN ARE VERY BRIGHT. YOU LEARN TO
UNDERSTAND WHAT THEY ARE THINKING ABOUT.
THEY KNOW WHAT THEY WANT IN LIFE. YOU HAVE TO
RESPECT THEIR SPACE. DON'T ASK TOO MANY QUESTIONS
BECAUSE THEY MAY NOT ANSWER THEM. THEIR MIND
IS ALWAYS BUSY. PEOPLE LOOK AT SPECIAL KIDS
AND SEE THEM AS DIFFERENT, AND THIS MAKES
THEM FEEL UNCOMFORTABLE.
YOU MUST CREATE A GOOD ENVIRONMENT
FOR THE SPECIAL CHILDREN.
                                    chaim

My Hero

We all have heroes
Those who take our breath away
For me it's my brother
Since his very first day.

We all have heroes
Who have grown against all odds
For me it's my brother
A special gift from G-d. special

We all have heroes
For whom it is difficult to adapt
For me it's my brother
Some may call him handicapped.

We all have heroes
Who play a leading role
For me it's my brother
And all of the hearts he stole.

We all have heroes
Who sing a different song
For me it's my brother
Because he lets me sing along.

We all have heroes
Whose music only they can hear
For me it's my brother
Every song is so dear

We all have heroes
Who can speak with great passion
For me it's my brother
He's small on talk and big on action.

We all have heroes
Who endure tribulations
For me it's my brother
He has taught me to be patient.

We all have heroes
With whom we share a dream
For me it's my brother
He is a part of our team.

We all have heroes
Who are stars of the show
For me it's my brother
It is a privilege to watch him grow.

We all have heroes
Whose road may be rough
For me it's my brother
Whose smile will always be enough.

We all have heroes
Who never show fear
For me it's my brother
And his unremitting cheer.

We all have heroes
Who have endured some pain
For me it's my brother
And all that he's gained.

We all have heroes
Whose challenges have been so real
For me it's my brother
And the sorrow I sometimes feel.

We all have heroes
Yours may look different than mine
For me it's my brother
Blue eyes with an everlasting shine.

We all have heroes
Yet as we get older they change
For me it's my brother
My hero, he does not age.

Rifky Zimlichman

A DAUGHTER SPEAKS OUT

On June 1ˢᵗ, my mother – Mrs. Judy Zimlichman – was a featured speaker at the FIRST CANADIAN CONFERENCE on SPECIAL EDUCATION for JEWISH CHILDREN held in Toronto. The title of her speech was 'A Mother's Journey'. As a pioneer in the special needs world of Montreal, she spoke about the difficulties and joys of raising my brother, Chaim. The following poem is a tribute to her. (JASE= Jewish Association for Special Education, in Montreal).

What a privilege it was to hear you speak, and inspire those whose futures seem bleak.

The trials, triumphs and tribulations of raising our brother, you imparted to a group that came to share with one another.

One thing you pondered and felt guilty about, was the fact that perhaps one of us felt left out.

Your energies were consumed night and day, occupied with Chaim's needs – could there be another way?

Well dear Mammy, there was no reason to fret, we never suffered from even one moment of neglect.

From a very young age, we were involved with our brother, our goal was that he be just like every other.

A child who will attend Yeshiva (school) and be accepted, from outside pain always protected.

Each day was a struggle so very real, but always a part of it we did feel.

No secret was kept, there was nothing to hide, amidst all the stares, we just stood there with pride.

A Family united, we had a mission, a goal; in 1980 JASE was born, and we were on a roll.

Working feverishly day in and day out, explaining to the world what we were all about.

A school to educate those who are in need of a special curriculum tailored to their very own speed.

Yes we remembered how occupied you became, and life was never exactly the same.

A constant flurry of phone calls and meetings galore, sometimes we wondered what's all this for?

But each waking moment we were reminded anew how privileged we are to have a mother like you.

Contrary to what you seem to remember, there was attention for every family member.

Our life was enriched and truly enhanced with each and every milestone – oh, how we danced!

From a very young age, you taught us about giving, an essential ingredient for a meaningful living.

We expected Chaim to be accepted by all, be it his classmates or just a game of ball.

We cheered Chaim on with every home run, isn't he also entitled to have fun?

There was lots of sharing, tears of frustration and joy, Chaim certainly wasn't an ordinary boy.

He could tell a joke, minus a detail or two, or recite all the current events he knew.

The skills Chaim mastered made it all worthwhile, we were always ready with a kiss, a hug and a smile.

Then one day – we were in a total state of shock, it was Chaim's Bar Mitzvah (the child who wasn't supposed to talk or walk!)

He lained (sang) his Haftara – the family began to weep, and delivered a dvar torah (speech) in Yiddish, there wasn't a peep.

For the crowd of hundreds just stood there totally amazed, for months afterwards he was constantly praised.

Moments like those made it worth our while, real gratification for going the extra mile.

Chaim davens, puts on tefillin, and learns how much he can, he has developed, and at twenty-one has become a man.

Looking back at the years, I could appreciate being part of a learning experience so great.

Were we ever deprived – having a sibling so dear? No Mammy, we weren't – so have no fear.

It taught us to accept that Hashem has a plan, we all have tests, and strengths that were given to man.

We must then discover the strength in our heart, daven to Hashem and try to do our part.

To my dear brother Chaim, I can't thank you enough, most certainly, there were times that seemed very tough.

I feel blessed because now I don't underestimate how each milestone in life is really so great.

I hope that you will continue being an important part of my new Family,

AM I MY BROTHER'S KEEPER? MOST DEFINITELY!!

Chaim Is His Name

"Limited potential," doctors were quick to proclaim.
He defied their predictions by far.
                    … Chaim is his name.

Igniting the spark, nurturing the flame.
Challenging, demanding, rewarding.
                    … Chaim is his name.

Step by step, that was the aim.
Each milestone celebrated with utmost gratification.
                    … Chaim is his name.

"But what about Chaim?" a common refrain.
The axis upon which family life rotated.
                    … Chaim is his name.

Genuine consideration for one and all, with no shame.
To friend or stranger, offering a heartfelt gesture.
                    … Chaim is his name.

Kindhearted to young and old, one and the same.
Warmth radiating to all with whom he connects.
                    … Chaim is his name.

Giving the shirt off his back is a literal claim.
His generosity and sincerity undisputed.
                    … Chaim is his name.

Far and wide, across the globe has spread his fame.
You will likely find those who've been inspired by
... Chaim is his name.

Of no misunderstandings is he to blame,
Because of the purest of his intentions.
... Chaim is his name.

Musical talents have won him acclaim,
Expressions of a special soul.
... Chaim is his name.

"Did you hear about ___?" he will often exclaim,
Sharing in others' happiness or sorrow.
... Chaim is his name.

Love and affection is the name of the game,
The language through which he relates.
... Chaim is his name.

I would never have been the same,
Had I not grown up with my brother.
... Chaim is his name.

Devorie Stolzman (Zimlichman), November 2010
(Toronto)

My Special Uncle
By: Esti Zoberman
Age 16

Every since I was young, I've had a special relationship with my Uncle Chaim. I was his first niece and I'd await his each and every visit with great anticipation. When I was small, I knew there was something different about Chaim but I couldn't quite put my foot on it yet.

When I was in first grade we used to have to write a journal. It was like a diary where we'd write something that was on our mind. I don't remember it clearly but my father constantly reminds me of my grade one journal entries. One of them apparently went something like this:

"I have an uncle named chaim and I love him very much. He comes to my house and kisses me a lot. My Tatty told me that Chaim can't get married and I think it's because he's too short." Obviously, chaim's inability to get to live without constant help has absolutely nothing to do with his height. However, at the tender age of six I could not understand what exactly mae my beloved uncle different than everyone else.

Until this day, chaim still askes us to be on the look out for a shidduch for him. If chaim tastes something delicious by a yom tov meal he'll ask us to make it for his sheva brachos. It is a constant struggle for cahim to see his younger cousins get married and his niece and nephew begin to drive for he knows this is something that is far from his reality.

We always enjoy chaim's visits to Toronto and love spernding time with him. He has a great sense of humour and is very sociable.

Over the years, I have done many school projects on chaim and have thought a lot about him and the way hne does things. We, all of chaim's nieces and nephews, love chaim very much and look forward to spending much quality time with him in the future years.

By: Chaim Zoberman
Age 8

Chaim is a very nice person. He is a very funny person. He wrote my favourite song. He is my favourite uncle. He gets the giggles. He lives in mason shalom.

The Differences About My Uncle
By: Moishe Zoberman
Age 10

I remember the times when my uncle would visit us. His jokes and his comments would make us laugh. He would put us in a good mood. He liked to put everyone in a good mood. He had his own way of doing things and it made everyone laugh. May be he zoche to lots more funny times.

Judy Zimlichman

My uncle Chaim is very special to me in many ways. He adds a lot to my life. Here are some examples; when I am around Chaim I feel a lot happier, since Chaim continuously spreads his פנימיות joy to everyone he comes in contact with. Although Chaim is very often happy he is also sometimes very worried. For example he is always making sure he has what to wear and eat, even if the pantrys and closets are full of food and clothing. Chaim is also very well known for his giggles; at times Chaim gets very hyper and could laugh and joke for hours on end. One of Chaim's best qualitys is his good voice. Chaim always enhances all our Shabbos and Yom tov meals by singing stunning songs. (As long as we promise him gumballs.) Furthermore Chaim loves babies and children and could always be found holding and kissing the babies. One funny story that comes to mind when I think about Chaim is when we took him to Yonkaale Shopping Mall. The first thing that Chaim wanted to buy was a present for his mother. Because of his heart of gold he walked into a diamond store and wanted to buy a diamond necklace for her. But because of Chaim's lack of understanding of the value of money he was ready to purchase the necklace. After my mother's strong convincing, Chaim reluctantly left and needed towards the chocolate store. Instead. At the chocolate store Chaim being the friendly person he is, took the plate of samples and went around the store offering them to the customers. (And if they refused his gracious offer he told them to take home for their children.) That's only one of the many stories about my favorite uncle, Chaim!

— Tova Stoltzman

68

Chaim My Uncle

C = Caring and considerate he always is to me.

H = he's my favorate uncle, he's close to me.

A = About everyone in his life he truly does care.

I = In all aspects of my daily life he wants me to share.

M = My favorite part about Chaim is he loves us unconditionally.

M = Mastered the techniques to reach into your heart.

Y = You know my day isn't complete without chatting to Chaim on the phone.

U = Uncle Chaim's whole focus in life centers on making people happy.

N = Nown for his contagous giggles.

C = constantly showing affection

L = Lots of feelings describe Chaim including his big heart, giving
E = personality, and his sensitivity for others.
Everyone will agree from the North Pole to over the big blue sea
that there's no one like my uncle Z. (zoe)

These are some thoughts that
come to mind when thinking
about Chaim.

By: Shira Stolzman
Toronto, Ontario

•

69

My best uncle Chaim

2003

I love uncle chaim. He is my best uncle.
I like chaim's jokes. He is very funny.
I like when he has the giggles.
Chaim is the best. You should treat him
better because he is handicap. He is a giver
because he saves us prizes that he wins in
work and gumballs. He has a good heart.
He loves his family more than anything in the
world. We take turns talking to uncle chaim each
day at dinner time. I am very proud of my
uncle chaim.

Me and Chaim

by Stuli Stolzman toronto canada 8 years old

Written by Tova and Yakov Blau

Uncle Chaim is different from other people. He acts different. He laughs different. But I still love him and he loves me.

Love, Tova

Uncle Chaim is handicapped, so that's why he acts differently than other people. He laughs differently than others, like when he cannot stop laughing for a long time. Uncle Chaim talks a little differently and laughs a lot at his own jokes. He also plays a little differently than other adults and enjoys playing children's games. But I love him a lot, and he likes me a lot. I like playing Connect Four with him and wrestling him. When we go on a trip, he is the most fun adult to play with. Even though he lives far away, I think about him and look forward to seeing him soon.

Love, Yakov

Written by Laye Goldstein Davidovitz (Chaim's Cousin)

There are so many things that I can remember that stand out, growing up with our cousin Chaim. However, his special way of being happy for others in their time of simcha truly stands out. The community can always count on Chaim, rain or shine, to come wish mazel tov for a special occasion.

Chaim's heart is so filled with love that he wants to participate in others' celebrations. Shabbos mornings begin with davening following a bris, kiddush, or *aufruf*. When you are happy, he laughs with you, and when you cry, he cries along too.

If one ever needs a *bracha*, there is no greater bracha available than one that is recited by Chaim. He is so attuned to what another person needs that the special words that leave his mouth pierce right through one's heart. I have often caught Chaim with tears in his eyes when giving us a bracha.

Even though he is limited in certain capacities, he is beyond capable when it comes to understanding other people's limitations and what Hashem can grant them.

Observations from the Social Worker's Perspective

Parenting a Special Child
Its Impact on the Family and the Community

Judy Zimlichman

*T*here have been thousands of books written about parenting special children. However, this one is unique, in that it bridges the personal and the professional experiences of families. For this reason, this book serves a unique purpose and fills a gap in the field.

When a parent is told that his or her child has a handicap (I will use this term also for a special need) or is challenged or will not develop normally, it feels as if lightning has hit you. The parent reels for days, weeks, or months from this shock and often does not know where to turn. A sort of emotional paralysis sets in sometimes because of the emotional shock. Furthermore, that parent may have other children, a job, and other stressors to tackle, and this news may be totally overwhelming at the moment.

An additional challenge for the family is when there is no clear diagnosis or prognosis. In such a case, the parent is unable to have clear expectations of the child, and it becomes difficult to plan for the future. The child may understand some things but not others. He may be able to understand some of the time but not all the time.

People react differently to having a baby with a handicap. Some may feel they will cope better by reaching out to community resources. Others may feel they will manage with help from family members and friends. While still others will feel they cannot cope with such a baby, and they may give the baby up for adoption or foster care. Some will see a special child as a gift from Hashem and a challenge. Others may see a handicapped child as a punishment for past sins. Some parents will be able to focus on the potential and the abilities of the child, while others will have difficulty seeing beyond the disabilities.

The care of a baby with a handicap may require special attention for feedings, doctor appointments, and therapies. This puts added pressure on family members, family time, and on the relationship between spouses. A single parent will face greater hardship in coping alone with all the demands of caring for a child with special needs.

Spouses have different ways of dealing with the emotional side of having a handicapped baby at home. They also deal differently with the extra caregiving stress that the special caregiving brings. One may feel that his heart is breaking from the pain, while the other may be ready to take on this new challenge with determination and hope for the future.

Parents and siblings of handicapped children can benefit greatly from the support of professionals who are experienced and knowledgeable in this field. They will also benefit from the support that their rabbi or clergyman can supply. Parents often feel lost in the new world of the special-needs child and its unique language. It is advisable to make contact with the social worker of the government community clinic. The pediatrician may also refer the baby to an early-intervention clinic for follow-up. Inquire about any services or subsidies that your family may be eligible for: food, diapers, respite services, babysitting, therapy, and counseling. Find out about assessments for the purpose of placement into preschool or application for residential-placement settings. Waiting lists can be very long for most services, so it is wise to put your child's name on as many lists as he may need in the future, as soon as possible. If you will not need a certain service, you always have the right to decline when they contact you. This is a sort of insurance policy so that your child will not have to wait nine to eighteen months for an evaluation. During long waits, the special child's problems may further deteriorate or become more complex. It is also possible that his self-esteem could decline with longer waits.

It is imperative that the child has a thorough medical and psychoeducational evaluation (if applicable), in order to help the professionals make a clear diagnosis (if possible). Such clarity allows everyone working with the child to have a good sense of direction regarding his therapy, education, behavior management, and parenting. Depending on the extent of the handicap, there may be a need for intervention in fine and gross motor skills, communication, education, or behavior modification. In the teenage years, the child may need family-life education and vocational training. These are only some of the possible areas in which a child may need assistance and support.

There must be a baseline evaluation (functional, psychological, intellectual) and annual follow-up to monitor the child's development. This evaluation can also be helpful to the professionals who work with the child on a daily basis and guide them in the direction they should take while working with the child. The short- and long-term goals are set by the professionals and the parents together so they all have common goals for the child.

A parent becomes the special child's advocate vis-à-vis the professionals, the community, and the government agencies. Parents would benefit from joining a support group of other parents who have a child of similar age and handicap, to get advice, share helpful resources, and brainstorm ideas.

As the child reaches school age, there will be discussions about integrating him into mainstream classes. It would be advisable for the parent to get the input of the educational psychologist to evaluate this and to determine if the child would benefit from integration or would do better in a special segregated school.

This is a very difficult problem for parents. The politically correct method is integration. However, some children lose out on an education because the mainstream system may not have enough resources to truly support a special-needs child. This decision is also dependent on the child's level of intellectual abilities, his behaviors, and his potential for social integration.

On the other hand, in a special school, the curriculum is specially tailored to the child's strengths and weaknesses, so the child can reach his maximum possible potential. The child's educational program is clearly outlined by the teachers and discussed with the parents at least twice a year. The plan is called an IEP (individual education plan) or ISP (individual service plan).

On the social level, a child who has a significant handicap cannot truly be integrated into activities with children the same age. The parent may send the child to a special school and seek out opportunities for the child to participate in social activities within their community. This way he will feel like part of the community in which he lives.

My advice to parents who wish to start a special education program in their community's day school is to seek the answer to the following question: Can the school truly support a special education program within its system? For a program of this type to succeed, it must be embraced fully, and the children must be integrated as much as possible into the larger school system. Financial arrangements need to be ironed out before an external organization sets up a program in a host school, to avoid disagreements later. The school has to see it as a privilege to house a special education program and not feel that it is doing a favor to parents, an outside organization, or the community.

Many of the existing special programs were established by parents who became vocal advocates because of their child with special educational needs. For such a program to be successful, the principal, the board members, and the rabbis or teachers of the school need to be sensitized and prepared how to embrace children with special needs into the educational and social structure of their school. On the high school level, some special-needs children need vocational training to enable them to do some meaningful work when they become young adults.

This needs to be supported morally and financially by the community leaders.

When a child with a mild handicap wants to do what any other normally developing child does, it may become a frustrating experience. This may continue throughout the teen years, when this child continues to measure himself against others and sees that he is coming up short. Other teens and young adults move on with their lives. The "special" child is left behind at every stage of life.

It may be less frustrating if the special child also has some friends who are special like him, so he can feel more normal in social settings. Joining a special program in a YMCA or a community center may be a good opportunity for him to meet other children and do things together.

Parents are often preoccupied with the immediate issues of day-to-day life. Just keeping up with daily demands may be effortful on some days when the parent is exhausted. When planning for the handicapped teenager, there must be multilayer planning for his future. His needs are like a puzzle with many pieces to be fitted together. The issues of education, prevocational training, life-skills training, family-life education, leisure activities, work, and social integration are just some of the pieces of the puzzle.

The difficult part of this exercise is that all the pieces of the puzzle need to be considered when a parent wants to make a decision about a single issue. At this stage of the child's life, the parents may have to accept the reality that the child may not meet all their early hopes and expectations. Parents must consider different options, some of which they may not have thought of in the past. The impact such decisions may have on the other children of the same family is a significant concern as well. This opens up a flood of emotions for the family, and it may be helpful to them to reach out for professional support and guidance.

With young adulthood new issues emerge regarding self-care needs, social opportunities, day programs, and quality of life. Meeting the child's physical and emotional needs may become more taxing as parents age, become more tired, and sometimes burn out. The question of placement of the special child or adult in a residential group home arises. Such a decision is very difficult emotionally. Parents, extended family members, and friends do not necessarily agree about the right course of action for the future of the special young adult.

Ultimately, one person needs to take responsibility for such a decision and help the special person adjust to the idea of his future. This is the time to enlist the help of a social worker to make the necessary applications.

It is common knowledge that there is a five- to ten-year wait list for placement in group homes. Preparing ahead of time is essential. If a place becomes available and parents decide not to accept the placement at that time, they can reconsider at a later time.

As special children become young adults, they may not be able to make important decisions for themselves. While we should involve them in discussions and decisions and try to give them some choices in life, at a certain age, moving out of the family home may become a reality.

For the young adult, living at home may be difficult because of social isolation and lack of meaningful activities. He may have greater difficulty moving out of the house at an older age. Some children may benefit from moving to a group home or to some other residential arrangement where there are social and recreational activities and greater independence. Parents can still be actively involved and take their child out on a regular basis for the day or for a weekend. Furthermore, they can advocate for their child who lives in a supportive environment.

Parents need to apply legally for curatorship by speaking with their child's social worker, so they can make the necessary decisions (medical, financial, and living environment) for their young-adult child. As legal representatives of the special child, they become future decision-makers for the person. These issues must be addressed and finalized before the child turns eighteen years old, to ensure a smooth process when it is required.

There are some families for whom the handicapped adult child becomes the caregiver to elderly parents. The welfare income of the handicapped adult may be an essential part of the family's income. At times the parents may want their handicapped adult to move to a residential setting, but the child does not want to. Such a situation is problematic both for the parents and for the handicapped adult. It is also potentially a situation for neglect and abuse within the family. The involvement of social services is valuable for long-term planning for all persons involved.

My Personal Trials and Tribulations

One of the most difficult times in my work happened in 1993, when the mandate of the special program we were running in the schools was terminated. In 1981, our association established the special education programs in two schools. The enrollment grew from six students to fifty-three students throughout the years, and it was seen as a model program by other schools to emulate. By 1993, the board members of the schools that were housing the special education resource rooms had come to the decision that they wanted to manage their own special education programs. This arrangement would allow the schools to use the special education money received from the government according to their own discretion. However, the end result turned out to be a different version of the old special education program.

Our association had clearly outlined the drawbacks of such a move: loss of quality of programming because

of a reduced amount of funds that would be allocated for the resource rooms, loss of income for the global special education program that was being raised by our association, and loss of objective quality control of the special education program in the resource rooms.

During the previous thirteen years, one of the most important roles our association played was being the only contact with the government in regards to the education of Jewish children with special needs. This role ensured a continuous and constant working relationship with the government, other schools, and community organizations.

In spite of hearing the above points, the schools proceeded with the transfer of the program. They incorporated all aspects of the special education program (administration, finances, and educational factors) into their own system.

I felt shattered by this experience. I was totally disappointed that members of the community were not willing to fight for the survival of our association. In thirteen years we created and developed something unique for the benefit of our special children; then it was just taken away. Our accomplishment was historically significant. For the very first time, it gave children with special needs in the community a voice, and the

opportunity to receive a Jewish special education within their community schools.

Starting in 1981, after the establishment of our association, I started working full time, but I had a flexible schedule, which allowed me to look after the children. My husband worked very long hours during the week and on Sundays as well. He was not able to be involved much with family life. As a result, I tried to balance my work and looking after the children at the same time. This was very stressful, and Chaim's special care created additional pressures for me.

The birth, development, and dissolution of our association was a personal journey as well as a professional journey for me. I learned a tremendous amount of information about how to deal with people, the government, and community organizations. I also had to learn how to communicate properly with parents and how to develop a professional persona of my own. There were many people who helped me along this journey, and I am forever grateful to them.

On a personal level, I have become more self-confident, resourceful, and knowledgeable about the issues of the special-needs population. I have also learned to accept my child totally and unconditionally. This acceptance allowed me to treat Chaim just like any of my other children when it came to love, discipline, and privileges.

As a result of my openness about parenting Chaim, I have received many phone calls from parents of children who need advice about some aspect of their special child's life. I enjoy helping other parents, and I hope my advice saves them some of the difficulties I had to endure. My goal is to share my thoughts and approaches with other parents and enable them to develop the skills required to make it work within the family and community context.

When a parent wants her special child integrated in the community shul or social programs, it is important that the child is socialized in a manner that allows him to fit into the existing community structure. If he knows how to behave in the shul, then others will accept him there just like they accept any other child. In return, the special child views this as a positive experience.

The desire to help other families who have special concerns prompted me to get involved as a volunteer with numerous organizations that serve people with special needs. I have spoken at conferences, assisted with organizational structuring, conducted parent groups, helped rewrite organizational constitutions for the government, raised funds, and written for their publications.

Whenever I am asked to get involved in helping families with handicapped children, I try to be as accommodating as possible. I remember vividly the way I felt when Chaim was born. I was isolated, lost, and had nowhere to turn for advice.

In 1993, a turning point in my life, I decided to return to school and complete my master's degree in the school of social work. I worked at a community clinic for twelve years. After that I was forced to stop working because of frequent and serious health problems. The many years of caring for others had finally caught up with me. To this day it continues to be a challenge for me to maintain my health.

Throughout my struggle with poor health, my first concern was always Chaim. How would he react to my sickness? It always made him very anxious to know I was ill, and he would worry about who would take care of him and his needs. Chaim is very attached to me. He wants a guarantee that I will be there for him forever and always.

EPILOGUE

Achieving the Impossible:
Looking Down from the Top of the Mountain

When I look back at the journey of the past thirty-nine years, a wave of mixed emotions flows through me. Those feelings of joy, achievement, gratitude, pain, hope, acceptance, and unfulfilled dreams have all been woven into one big collage.

The sense of accomplishment and joy is overwhelming, and it makes one want to forget all the difficult times that transpired during the journey.

==

2012—(View from the Mountaintop) First-Person Notes

Chaim has been living in the group home for the past fifteen years. He comes home (to his parents) every weekend.

He brings joy and love into our lives. When he steps into the house on Friday afternoons, his big blue eyes are dancing, his body is in constant motion, and he loves to take a tour around the house each time he comes home. He feels a sense of security, knowing that everything and everyone is all right.

After settling down, he is excited to talk about his week and all his activities. He speaks clearly, and his choice of words is amazing. At times we are left speechless listening to him talk about current affairs, community issues, or interpersonal relationships. In spite of his limited intelligence, his language abilities are amazing. He can join in a discussion around the table and hold his own, but he has difficulty understanding when to stop.

On the other hand, we love to hear him sing and to sing with him for hours on end. He seems transported to another planet when he sings from his heart. With his eyes closed and his body relaxed, he sways to the melody, seems to connect with some higher inspiration, and is oblivious to the world around him. After such a performance, he feels proud of himself. Those are the times I feel that he brought so much joy into our lives with his presence.

As I look at him, my heart swells with pride at how well he manages himself. I feel that he has become a mensch. His sensitivity to others is exceptional. At his group home, he has a kind word or a hug for any of the other residents who may be having a difficult time.

When he arrives home, he takes one look at my face and is able to tell how I am feeling. Even though at times I don't want to tell him if I am not well, he senses it and tells me his observations.

Final Thoughts—First-Person Notes

Present

He is a thirty-nine-year-old young man. His name is Chaim, which means *life*. He does not look his age; he looks more like a teenage boy. He has huge blue eyes and a smile that lights up the room. It is Friday afternoon. He greets everyone when he enters the room, and they greet him warmly. He is their friend. He feels at home in the place. He checks out his friends' ties and the buttons on their coats. He seems a bit unusual, but he fits seamlessly into this environment. He's known the people in this place for about thirty years. They understand his being different and accept him the way he is. He feels loved here in this synagogue. When he arrives home to start the Friday evening meal, he sings his favorite songs and shares the happenings from his week. He talks about his dreams and his wishes to get married sometime, just as his friends did. We try lovingly to encourage him to enjoy life and to thank Hashem for all the loving friends and family he has.

He has been challenging us throughout the past thirty-nine years to accept him and love him unconditionally, and he has taught us to appreciate every small thing in life.

Looking at Chaim's life gives me the feeling that we are participants in a play that is written and directed by a higher power. However, no one knows the whole script and cannot envision how the play will end.

Chaim's presence on earth changed many lives for the better, and he continues to inspire and touch other people with his special love and humor. As time goes by, I have come to realize more and more that to appreciate the journey we are part of is what's important, not the destination.

===

Chaim is the epicenter of our lives and gives us much joy and love. He is intellectually handicapped but physically independent. He loves people, and people love him back. He says many times that he is happy that people like him and accept him, even though he is handicapped.

Chaim has good language skills, an exceptional memory, a good sense of humor, and loves music and singing. He is an integral part of all our family visits and get-togethers. Chaim moved to the group home at the age of twenty-two, and he is happy to be a part of that family also. He spends Shabbos and holidays with us at our home. We speak to him at least twice a day, every day. He comes with us out of town every time we go to visit his sisters. We could not imagine our lives without him. As a result of parenting Chaim, we have become more sensitive and have learned a tremendous amount about life. It has been a challenge that has brought with it opportunities for wisdom and spiritual growth and enabled me to help other people who have children with special needs.

PARENTS' CODE OF RIGHTS

*M*any professionals talk about parents going through something called "the grieving process" when they learn of their child's handicap. According to this theory, parents first go through a stage of shock. This is followed by a sense of sorrow or grief, where parents are thought to mourn for the loss of the "perfect" child that most parents hope for and expect. Then comes denial, where parents deny that their child is really handicapped, or perhaps seek out other doctors to get second, third, and fourth opinions. Anger and resentment come next, and then, finally, comes acceptance.

These stages - shock, grief, denial, anger, and acceptance — are often used by the professionals who interact with you and your family to describe your feelings and sometimes your actions. The grieving process is only a theory, but it is widely believed, perhaps because it helps the professionals deal with your feelings. (It is easier to see similarities among people than it is, sometimes, to see the individual.) You may, in fact, have all these feelings. But you also have certain rights:

1. THE RIGHT TO FEEL ANGRY

   Nothing in life prepares anyone for being handicapped, and when it is your child who is handicapped, it seems all the more unfair. You did not ask for this, and there is very little you can do to change it. Your sense of control over your own life and the life of your child is at risk. Be angry, but use your anger to get the best services you can for your child.

2. THE RIGHT TO SEEK ANOTHER OPINION

   Everyone is told today that it makes good sense to seek a second opinion before having surgery, or before investing money, or before buying a used car. It should not be any different for you and your handicapped child, whether you are looking for medical care or an educational program. If you hear of a new treatment that might help your child, why shouldn't you look into it?

3. THE RIGHT TO PRIVACY

Many parents have talked about the effects a handicapped child in the family has on family members' privacy, because a handicapped child suddenly brings into the family circle a series of professionals who examine, give advice, and sometimes even judge the actions of individual family members. One parent said that the hardest part for her was "having to turn to experts". It was difficult having to have someone "tell me what to do with my child". Some aspects of your life are simply no one else's business. If you do not want to discuss something, or if you do not want your child's picture taken, it is your right to say "No".

4. THE RIGHT TO KEEP TRYING

Parenting is not easy, but all parents try to do the best job they can. It sometimes becomes harder when well-meaning friends and professionals tell you that you have set goals that your child will never be able to reach, or that you must stand back and accept the fact your daughter is multiply handicapped and will never be able to walk. There is nothing wrong with you if you are not willing to give up. Your child has the greatest potential for learning now, in the preschool years, and no one knows what event or combination of events will make a difference for her. If the others turn out to be right - so what? You will have given your child the best chance she could have.

5. THE RIGHT TO STOP TRYING

Well-meaning friends and professionals have also told parents that they do not work often enough or long enough with their handicapped children. "If you would just do this at home for 15 minutes a day on the weekends, it would make such a difference". The truth is that it could just as easily make no difference at all. You are the one who lives with your child; you are the one who is being asked to do one more thing; you are the one who is somehow expected to accomplish at home what trained teachers have not been able to do at school. If you just cannot do it tonight — okay. That is your decision.

6. THE RIGHT TO SET LIMITS

There are limits to what one person can do; you shouldn't expect yourself to think about your child all the time. And your child shouldn't expect to be the centre of attention. You have limits, and your child has limits: learn to recognize both, and give yourself a chance to examine the situation before responding in anger or fatigue. You are not superparent.

7. THE RIGHT TO BE A PARENT

    Teachers who work with young handicapped children and their families are fond of giving parents activities to do at home. But you are mommy and daddy first. You cannot expect to be a teacher all the time, and even your child's teacher cannot teach all the time. (If you ask her teacher, he will probably admit that he is great at teaching other people's kids, but he can't do a thing with his own.) You and your child need time to fool around, giggle, tickle, tell stories, laugh, and just do nothing. Those times are an important part of your child's "education".

8. THE RIGHT TO BE UNENTHUSIASTIC

    No one expects you to be "turned on" all the time. Sometimes you feel sad, or you're worried about money, or your child, or you feel sick. If other people take that as a sign that you're "not adjusting" or that you're "not accepting your child's handicap", that is their problem. No one is excited about work every day; it can be tedious one day and new and interesting the next. The same is true of parenting. There will be days when your child thrills you with joy and days when parenting will seem like the most boring job on earth. You have a right to be "up" sometimes and "down" others.

9. THE RIGHT TO BE ANNOYED WITH
YOUR CHILD

There are days when you like your child and days when you don't, but that does not mean that you don't love her. Children with Cerebral Palsy are just as capable of being ornery as other children, and they should be disciplined as any other children.

10. THE RIGHT TO TIME OFF

You need time to yourself, time with your spouse or partner and other adult family members, and just plain time without kids. Many parents describe the first time they went to the grocery store alone after their child was born as a tremendous feeling of freedom, even though they were doing a chore, and even though they didn't talk to anyone but the check-out clerk. There are many parts to your life, and each deserves as much attention and nurturing as does your special needs child.

11. THE RIGHT TO BE THE
EXPERT-IN-CHARGE

You know your child better than anyone else: You spend the most time with him/her, you have lived with her longer than anyone else, you know what works and what doesn't. Teachers come and go, but you are the expert with the experience and first-hand knowledge about your child. And, as the expert, you have the right to be in charge of your child's educational, social and medical decisions — at least until she is able to make them herself. Professionals do not live with the consequences of their decisions, so while you might want their opinions, remember that they are only opinions and not facts. They cannot tell you you're wrong, that you will regret it, that you're selfish, or that you're not looking far enough ahead. Nor can they make you feel guilty or pressure you into a decision. Parents are the single most important resource that children have.

12. THE RIGHT TO DIGNITY

These rights of parents really boil down to the right to be respected and treated as an equal. You expect to be neither pitied nor admired, but you do expect to be listened to and taken seriously. You expect to be treated as though your child were not handicapped. You expect the truth — from the doctors, teachers, social workers and therapists, who are there to help you; from your friends and neighbours, who owe you a chance to be someone other than "parent-of-a-handicapped-child"; and from your family members, who love you. You deserve the courtesy of having professionals, who visit you at your home arrive promptly for appointments. If a teacher is repeatedly late and does not have a satisfactory excuse, call the program supervisor and ask why. You deserve to be talked to as an adult; if you feel a teacher or a therapist is talking down to you, tell him so. Sometimes, when you are the parent of a handicapped child, you have to risk being aggressive and, sometimes, even rude, in order to obtain the dignity that is your right and your due.

None of these 12 rights apply just to parents of handicapped children; all parents share certain common experiences, whether they have one child or 10, and whether one child or all 10 are handicapped. You cannot forget that you are an adult with your own needs, desires, hopes and dreams. Enjoy your individuality and enjoy your child.

Adapted from and reprinted by permission of American Foundation for the Blind, New York.

....FORGET – ME – NOT ....

Our problems are and varied.

Our struggles are always uphill.

I'am speaking for hundreds of children.

So listen a while if you will.

I want understanding - not pity.

I wish you could treat me the same.

You would not ignore other children.

At least you would ask them their name.

I know I can't answer to tell you.

My face may seem empty and dead.

My body is twisted – but I am alive.

And there are thoughts in my head.

I will not be shut out from the world.

I'am a child and it is my right,

I'am not an object of pity –

To be hidden away out of sight.

My parents see me through eyes of love.

And not as others do.

They see the things I can achieve.

And I wish that you would too.

As I ask you to forget-me-not,

I beg you to hear my plea

If I could speak – I would ask you

To please look closer – and see me....

The Ten Commandments For Parents Of Special Needs Children

1. Take one day at a time, and take that day positively. You don't have control over the future, over today, or over any other day, and neither does anyone else. Other people just think they do.

2. Never underestimate your child's potential. Allow him, encourage him, and expect him to develop to the best of his abilities.

3. Find and allow positive mentors: parents and professionals who can share with you their experience, advice, and support.

4. Provide and be involved with the most appropriate educational and learning environments for your child from infancy on.

5. Keep in mind the feelings and needs of your spouse and your other children. Remind them that this child does not get more of your love just because he gets more of your time.

6. Answer only to your conscience: then you'll be able to answer to your child. You need not justify your actions to your friends or the public.

7. Be honest with your feelings. You can't be a super-parent 24 hours a day. Allow yourself jealousy, anger, pity, frustration, and depression in small amounts whenever necessary.

8. Be kind to yourself. Don't focus continually on what needs to be done. Remember to look at what you have accomplished.

9. Stop and smell the roses. Take advantage of the fact that you have gained a special appreciation for the little miracles in life that others take for granted.

10. Keep and use a sense of humor. Cracking up with laughter can keep you from cracking up from stress.

This refrigerator door item thanks to the Children's Special Health Care Needs Mailing List, (CSHN-L) sponsored by the University of Florida's Institute for Child Study.]

HEAVEN'S VERY SPECIAL CHILD

A meeting was held quite far from earth,
"It's time again for another birth,"
Said the Angels to the Lord above,
"This special child will need much love.

His progress may seem very slow
Accomplishments he may not show
And he'll require extra care
From the folks he meets way down there.

He may not run or laugh or play
His thoughts may seem quite far away
In many ways he won't adapt,
And he will be known as handicapped.

So let's be careful where he's sent
We want his life to be content.
Please, Lord, find the parents who
Will do a special job for You.

They will not realize right away
The leading role they're asked to play
But with this child sent from above
Comes stronger faith and richer love.

And soon they will know the privilege given
In caring for this gift from Heaven.
Their precious charge, so meek and mild,
is Heaven's very special child.

GLOSSARY OF JEWISH WORDS

alliyah	an honor; to be called up to the Torah
baal tefilah	leader of prayer services
Badchen	Jewish comedian with scholarly overtones
bar mitzvah	thirteen-year-old male celebrates becoming a man according to Jewish law
bracha	blessing
bris	Jewish circumcision
chavrusa	a pair of students learning together Jewish texts
davening	praying
dvar Torah	speaking fascinating insights from the Torah
frum	a Jew who is committed to the strict observance of Jewish laws

haftarah	selected texts from the Torah
halacha	Jewish religious law
Hashem	God
kibbutz	a communal settlement (farm) in Israel
kiddush	blessing on a cup of wine on Shabbat
mazel/mazel tov	luck, good luck
minyan (minyonim)	quorum of Jewish men over thirteen years old required for public prayer
mitzvah/mitzvos	commandments by God; a moral deed performed as a religious duty
neshama	Jewish soul, spirit
pshetl	speech about a topic in the Torah
rav	rabbi, religious leader
rebbe	teacher of Torah
schiduch (shiduchim)	matchmaking for the purpose of marriage
Shabbat	Judaism's day of rest; seventh day of the week
shalosh seudos	third meal during Shabbat (late afternoon)
shiur (shiurim)	a lecture/lesson on a Torah subjects
shul	prayer hall; synagogue

siddur (siddurim)	prayer book(s)
simcha	joy, gladness
Simchas Torah	holiday celebrating the rejoicing with the Torah scrolls
tefillin	black leather phylacteries worn by observant Jews during daily morning prayers
Torah	the central reference of the religious Judaic tradition
tzitzis	ritual white shirt with tassels worn by religious Jewish men
yarmulke	skullcap
yeshiva	Jewish religious educational institution focused on Torah studies
Yom Tov (Yomim Tovim)	Jewish holiday(s)
zmiros	melody, song

PHOTO GALLERY

1976 Chaim is 3 months old here

1978 Chaim and his family

1979 Chaim and his sisters with grandparents

1979 Chaim

1983 Chaim with a friend

1984 Chaim learning to ride a bike
with his grandfather's help

1993 Chaim in Camp HASC

1993 Chaim with two of his sisters

1994 Chaim with two of his brother-in-laws

1994 Chaim's birthday at Maison Shalom

1995 Chaim with his sisters

1996 Chaim with his boss, Mr. Alex
Patterson, at McMaster Meighen

1997 Chaim graduating from Summit School

1997 Chaim with his aunt

2000 Chaim dancing with his youngest sister

2000 Chaim with his father

2003 Chaim with nieces

2006 Chaim recording his CD

2007

2008

2009 Chaim with his little niece

2009 Chaim with his nephew and nieces

2009 Chaim with one of his sisters

2009 Chaim withn his sister Devoirie

2010 Chaim with his sister and brother-in-law

2011

2012 Chaim with his mother

2012 Chaim with his sister Devoirie

2012 Chaim with his sister

2012 Chaim with his youngest sister

2013 Chaim dressed for masquerade

2014 Chaim with his oldest nephew

2015 Chaim baking

ADDENDUM I

July 8, 2007

The Gregarious Brain

By DAVID DOBBS

If a person suffers the small genetic accident that creates Williams syndrome, he'll live with not only some fairly conventional cognitive deficits, like trouble with space and numbers, but also a strange set of traits that researchers call the Williams social phenotype or, less formally, the "Williams personality": a love of company and conversation combined, often awkwardly, with a poor understanding of social dynamics and a lack of social inhibition. The combination creates some memorable encounters. Oliver Sacks, the neurologist and author, once watched as a particularly charming 8-year-old Williams girl, who was visiting Sacks at his hotel, took a garrulous detour into a wedding ceremony. "I'm afraid she disrupted the flow of this wedding," Sacks told me. "She also mistook the bride's mother for the bride. That was an awkward moment. But it very much pleased the mother."

Video

More Video »

Another Williams encounter: The mother of twin Williams boys in their late teens opened her door to find on her stoop a leather-clad biker, motorcycle parked at the curb, asking for her sons. The boys had made the biker's acquaintance via C.B. radio and invited him to come by, but they forgot to tell Mom. The biker visited for a spell. Fascinated with how the twins talked about their condition, the biker asked them to speak at his motorcycle club's next meeting. They did. They told the group of the genetic accident underlying Williams, the heart and vascular problems that eventually kill many who have it, their intense enjoyment of talk, music and story, their frustration in trying to make friends, the slights and cruelties they suffered growing up, their difficulty understanding the world. When they finished, most of the bikers were in tears.

142

These stories are typical of those who have Williams syndrome. (Some people with the disorder as well as many who work with them simply call it Williams.) Williams syndrome rises from a genetic accident during meiosis, when DNA's double helix is divided into two separate strands, each strand then becoming the genetic material in egg or sperm. Normally the two strands part cleanly, like a zipper's two halves. But in Williams, about 25 teeth in one of the zippers — 25 genes out of 30,000 in egg or sperm — are torn loose during this parting. When that strand joins another from the other parent to eventually form an embryo, the segment of the DNA missing those 25 genes can't do its work.

The resulting cognitive deficits lie mainly in the realm of abstract thought. Many with Williams have so vague a concept of space, for instance, that even as adults they will fail at six-piece jigsaw puzzles, easily get lost, draw like a preschooler and struggle to replicate a simple T or X shape built with a half-dozen building blocks. Few can balance a checkbook. These deficits generally erase about 35 points from whatever I.Q. the person would have inherited without the deletion. Since the average I.Q. is 100, this leaves most people with Williams with I.Q.'s in the 60s. Though some can hold simple jobs, they require assistance managing their lives.

The low I.Q., however, ignores two traits that define Williams more distinctly than do its deficits: an exuberant gregariousness and near-normal language skills. Williams people talk a lot, and they talk with pretty much anyone. They appear to truly lack social fear. Indeed, functional brain scans have shown that the brain's main fear processor, the amygdala, which in most of us shows heightened activity when we see angry or worried faces, shows no reaction when a person with Williams views such faces. It's as if they see all faces as friendly.

People with Williams tend to lack not just social fear but also social savvy. Lost on them are many meanings, machinations, ideas and intentions that most of us infer from facial expression, body language, context and stock phrasings. If you're talking with someone with Williams syndrome and look at your watch and say: "Oh, my, look at the time! Well it's been awfully nice talking with you . . . ," your conversational partner may well smile brightly, agree that "this is nice" and ask if you've ever gone to Disney World. Because of this — and because many of us feel uneasy with people with cognitive disorders, or for that matter with anyone profoundly unlike us — people with Williams can have trouble deepening relationships. This saddens and frustrates them. They know no strangers but can claim few friends.

This paradox — the urge to connect, the inability to fully do so — sits at the center of the Williams puzzle, whether considered as a picture of human need (who hasn't been shut out of a circle he'd like to join?) or, as a growing number of researchers are finding, a clue to the fundamental drives and tensions that shape social behavior. After being ignored for almost three decades, Williams has recently become one of the most energetically researched neurodevelopmental disability after autism, and it is producing more compelling insights. Autism, for starters, is a highly diverse "spectrum disorder" with ill-defined borders, no identified mechanism and no clearly delineated genetic basis. Williams, in contrast, arises from a known genetic cause and produces a predictable set of traits and behaviors. It is "an experiment of nature," as the title of one paper puts it, perfect for studying not just how genes create intelligence and sociability but also how our powers of thought combine with our desire to bond to create complex social behavior — a huge arena of interaction that largely determines our fates.

Julie R. Korenberg, a neurogeneticist at Cedars-Sinai Medical Center and at the University of California, Los Angeles, who has helped define the Williams deletion and explore its effects, believes the value of Williams syndrome in examining such questions is almost impossible to overstate. "We've long figured that major behavioral traits rose in indirect fashion from a wide array of genes," Korenberg says. "But here we have this really tiny genetic deletion — of the 20-some-odd genes missing, probably just 3 to 6 create the cognitive and social effects — that reliably creates a distinctive behavioral profile. Williams isn't just a fascinating mix of traits. It is the most compelling model available for studying the genetic bases of human behavior."

Korenberg's work is part of a diverse research effort on Williams that is illuminating a central dilemma of human existence: to survive we must relate and work with others, but we must also compete against them, lest we get left behind. It's like the TV show "Survivor": we want to keep a place in the group — we must — and doing so requires not only charming others but also showing we can contribute to their success. This requires a finely calibrated display of smarts, savvy, grit and hustle. Show too little, and you're voted off the island for being subpar. Show too much, and you're ousted as a conniving threat.

Where is the right balance? A partial answer lies in the mix of skills, charms and deficiencies that is Williams syndrome.

Williams syndrome was first identified in 1961 by Dr. J. C. P. Williams of New Zealand. Williams, a cardiologist at Greenlane Hospital in Auckland, noticed that a number of the hospital's young cardiac patients were small in stature, had elfin facial features and seemed friendly but in some ways were mentally slow. His published delineation of this syndrome put Dr. Williams on the map — off which he promptly and mysteriously fell. Twice offered a position at the prestigious Mayo Clinic in Rochester, Minn., he twice failed to show, disappearing the second time, in the late '60s, from London, his last known location, with the only trace an unclaimed suitcase later found in a luggage office.

The rarity of Williams syndrome — about 1 in 7,500 people have it, compared with about 1 in 150 for autism or 1 in 800 for Down syndrome — rendered it obscure. Unless they had the syndrome's distinctive cardiovascular problems (which stem from the absence of the gene that makes blood vessels, heart valves and other tissue elastic and which even today limit the average lifespan of a person with Williams to around 50), most people with Williams were simply considered "mentally retarded."

This ended in the late 1980s, when a few researchers in the emerging field of cognitive neuroscience began to explore Williams. Among the most earnest was Ursula Bellugi, the director of the Laboratory for Cognitive Neuroscience at the Salk Institute for Biological Studies in La Jolla, Calif. Bellugi, who specializes in the neurobiology of language, was drawn to the linguistic strength that many Williamses displayed in the face of serious cognitive problems. The first person with Williams she met, in fact, came by referral from the linguist Noam Chomsky.

"The mother of that Williams teenager later connected me with two more, both in their teens," Bellugi said. "I didn't have to talk to them long to realize something special was going on. Here they had these great cognitive deficits. Yet they spoke with the most ardent and delightful animation and color."

To understand this uneven cognitive profile, Bellugi gave an array of language and cognitive tests to three groups: Williams children and teenagers, Down syndrome kids with similar I.Q.'s and developmentally average peers. "We would do these warm-up interviews to get to know them, ask about their families," said Bellugi, who, less than five feet tall and with a ready smile and an animated manner, is somewhat elfin and engagingly gregarious herself. "Only, the Williams kids would turn the tables. They'd tell you how pretty you look or ask, 'Do you like opera?' They would ornament their answers in a way other kids didn't. For instance, you'd ask an adolescent, 'What if you were a bird?' The Down kids said things like: 'I'm not a bird. I don't fly.' The Williams teens would say: 'Good question! I'd fly through the air being free. If I saw a boy I'd land on his head and chirp.' "

Bellugi found that this fanciful verbosity was accompanied by infectious affability. To measure it she developed a questionnaire and gave it to parents of Williams, Down and normal children. It asked about things like friendliness toward strangers, connections to familiar people, different social scenarios. At every age level, those with Williams scored significantly higher in sociability than those in the other groups. Having long studied the human capacity for language and its biological basis, Bellugi assumed that some extraordinary urge to use language drove this hypersociability: "The language just seemed to be erupting out of them."

Then she attended a meeting of Williams families that included infants and toddlers. "That was about a year into my research project," she says. "The room was full of little ones — babies, toddlers who weren't speaking yet. And when I came in the room all the young children old enough to walk ran to the door to greet me. No clinging to Mom; they just broke away. And when I would talk to mothers holding infants — literally babes in arms — some of these babies would almost dive out of their mothers' arms to meet me.

"I knew then I was wrong. The language wasn't driving the sociability. If anything, it was the other way around."

Developmental psychologists sometimes call the social urge the "drive to affiliate." It seemed clear early on that the Williams deletion, which was definitively identified in the mid-1990s, either strengthened this drive or left it unfettered. But how do missing genes steer behavior toward gregariousness and engagement? How can a deletion heighten a trait rather than diminish it?

I got a hint when I met Nicki Hornbaker, who is 19, at Bellugi's office in La Jolla. Nicki, whose Williams was diagnosed when she was 2, has been participating as a subject in Bellugi's research for 15 years. She and her mother, Verna, drove down from Fresno that day to continue testing and to talk with me about living with Williams syndrome. Like most people with Williams, Nicki loves to talk but has trouble getting past a cocktail-party-level chatter. Nicki, however, has fashioned at least a partial solution.

"Ever since she was tiny," Verna Hornbaker told me, "Nicki has always especially loved to talk to men. And in the last few years, by chance, she figured out how to do it. She reads the sports section in the paper, and she watches baseball and football on TV, and she has learned enough about this stuff that she can talk to any man about what the 49ers or the Giants are up to. My husband gets annoyed when I say this, but I don't mean it badly: men typically have that superficial kind of conversation, you know — weather and sports. And Nicki can do it. She knows what team won last night and where the standings are. It's only so deep. But she can do it. And she can talk a good long while with most men about it."

In the view of two of Bellugi's frequent collaborators, Albert Galaburda, a Harvard Medical School professor of neurology and neuroscience, and Allan Reiss, a neuroscientist at the Stanford School of Medicine, Nicki's learned facility at sports talk illustrates a central lesson of Williams and, for that matter, modern genetics: genes (or their absence) do not hard-wire people for certain behaviors. There is no gene for understanding calculus. But genes do shape behavior and personality, and they do so by creating brain structures and functions that favor certain abilities and appetites more than others.

Reiss and Galaburda's imaging and autopsy work on Williamses' brains, for instance, has shown distinct imbalances in structure and synaptic connectivity. This work has led Galaburda to suspect that some of the genes missing in the Williams deletion are "patterning genes," which direct embryonic development and which in this case dictate brain formation. Work in lab animals has shown that at least one patterning gene choreographs the developmental balance between the brain's dorsal areas (along the back and the top of the brain) and ventral areas (at the front and bottom). The dorsal areas play a strong role in vision and space and help us recognize other peoples' intentions; ventral areas figure heavily in language, processing sounds, facial recognition, emotion, music enjoyment and social drive. In an embryo's first weeks, Galaburda says, patterning genes normally moderate "a sort of turf war going on between these two areas," with each trying to expand. The results help determine our relative strengths in these areas. We see them in our S.A.T. scores, for example: few of us score the same in math (which draws mostly on dorsal areas) as in language (ventral), and the discrepancy varies widely. The turf war is rarely a draw.

In Williams the imbalance is profound. The brains of people with Williams are on average 15 percent smaller than normal, and almost all this size reduction comes from underdeveloped dorsal regions. Ventral regions, meanwhile, are close to normal and in some areas — auditory processing, for example — are unusually rich in synaptic connections. The genetic deletion predisposes a person not just to weakness in some functions but also to relative (and possibly absolute) strengths in others. The Williams newborn thus arrives facing distinct challenges regarding space and other abstractions but primed to process emotion, sound and language.

This doesn't mean that specific behaviors are hard-wired. M.I.T. math majors aren't born doing calculus, and people with Williams don't enter life telling stories. As Allan Reiss put it: "It's not just 'genes make brain make behavior.' You have environment and experience too."

By environment, Reiss means less the atmosphere of a home or a school than the endless string of challenges and opportunities that life presents any person starting at birth. In Williams, he says, these are faced by someone who struggles to understand space and abstraction but readily finds reward listening to speech and looking at faces. As the infant and toddler seeks and prolongs the more rewarding experiences, already-strong neural circuits get stronger while those in weaker areas may atrophy. Patterns of learning and behavior follow accordingly.

"Take the gaze," Reiss told me. Everyone who has worked with Williams children knows the Williams gaze, which in toddlers is often an intense, penetrating eye contact of the sort described as "boring right through you." The gaze can seem like a hard-wired expression of a Williams's desire to connect. Yet the gaze can also be seen as a skill learned at the end of the horrible colic that many Williams infants suffer during their first year and before they start to talk well. This window is longer than that for most infants, as Williams children, oddly, start talking a year or so later than most children. It's during this window that the gaze is at its most intense. Until she was 9 months old, for instance, Nicki Hornbaker rarely slept more than an hour at a time, and when she was quiet she tended to look vaguely at her mother's hairline. Then her colic stopped, she started sleeping and "almost overnight," her mother told me, "she became a happy, delightful, extremely social child, and she couldn't get enough eye contact." Later, when talk gave Nicki a more effective way to connect, the intensity of the eye contact eased. Nicki's eyes now meet yours, warm and engaging, but they don't bore through you.

To Reiss, the gaze is one of several things Williams people learn in order to pursue social connections. "They want that connection," he said, "and they learn all these things to get it: the gaze and the gregariousness, the smiles and

146

language and narrative skills, in succession as they're able to. What they learn is shaped by the inclinations and abilities their genes create.

"Look at the difference between Williams kids and fragile X." Fragile X, another developmental syndrome, produces similar cognitive defects but a pronounced social reticence or aversion to looking at faces. If a Williams wants to lock eyes, a fragile X child will literally twist himself sideways to avoid eye contact. "Nothing could be more different from a Williams," Reiss continued. "But the thing is, fragile X kids don't do that when they're a year old. They'll still look at you at that age. And Williams kids don't have that intense gaze yet at that age. It's only over the next year or two that they take this incredible divergence. In both cases you have a genetically inclined pattern of behavior that is reinforced."

This is a genetic version of Bellugi's observation that sociability drives language. The child gravitates toward the pathways that offer smoother going or more interesting experiences — at least until she finds other pathways more rewarding (sports talk, for example). In fragile X, those pathways tend to keep a child close to himself. In Williams they lead headlong toward others.

As an experiment of nature, Williams syndrome makes clear that while we are innately driven to connect with others, this affiliative drive alone will not win this connection. People with Williams rarely win full acceptance into groups other than their own. To bond with others we must show not just charm but sophisticated cognitive skills. But why? For vital relationships like those with spouses or business partners, the answer seems obvious: people want to know you can contribute. But why should casual friendships and group membership depend on smarts?

One possible answer a comes from the rich literature of nonhuman primate studies. For 40 years or so, primatologists like Jane Goodall, Frans de Waal and Robert Sapolsky have been studying social behavior in chimps, gorillas, macaques, bonobos and baboons. Over the past decade that work has led to a unifying theory that explains not only a huge range of behavior but also why our brains are so big and what their most essential work is. The theory, called the Machiavellian-intelligence or social-brain theory, holds that we rise from a lineage in which both individual and group success hinge on balancing the need to work with others with the need to hold our own — or better — amid the nested groups and subgroups we are part of.

It started with fruit. About 15 or 20 million years ago, the theory goes, certain forest monkeys in Africa and Asia developed the ability to digest unripe fruit. This left some of their forest-dwelling cousins — the ancestors of chimps, gorillas and humans — at a sharp disadvantage. Suddenly a lot of fruit was going missing before it ripened.

To find food, some of the newly hungry primate species moved to the forest edge. Their new habitat put more food in reach, but it also placed the primates within reach of big cats, canines and other savanna predators. This predation spurred two key evolutionary changes. The primates became bigger, giving individuals more of a fighting chance, and they started living in bigger groups, which provided more eyes to keep watch and a strength of numbers in defense.

But the bigger groups imposed a new brain load: the members had to be smart enough to balance their individual needs with those of the pack. This meant cooperating and exercising some individual restraint. It also required understanding the behavior of other group members striving not only for safety and food but also access to mates.

147

And it called for comprehending and managing one's place in an ever-shifting array of alliances that members formed in order not to be isolated within the bigger group.

How did primates form and manage these alliances? They groomed one another. Monkeys and great apes spend up to a fifth of their time grooming, mostly with regular partners in pairs and small groups. This quality time (grooming generates a pleasing release of endorphins and oxytocin) builds strong bonds. Experiments in which a recording of macaques screaming in alarm is played, for instance, have shown a macaque will respond much more strongly to a grooming partner's cries than to cries from other members of the group. The large time investment involved seems to make a grooming relationship worth defending.

In this and other ways a group's members would create, test and declare their alliances. But as the animals and groups grew, tracking and understanding all those relationships required more intelligence. According to the social-brain theory, it was this need to understand social dynamics — not the need to find food or navigate terrain — that spurred and rewarded the evolution of bigger and bigger primate brains.

This isn't idle speculation; Robin Dunbar, an evolutionary psychologist and social-brain theorist, and others have documented correlations between brain size and social-group size in many primate species. The bigger an animal's typical group size (20 or so for macaques, for instance, 50 or so for chimps), the larger the percentage of brain devoted to neocortex, the thin but critical outer layer that accounts for most of a primate's cognitive abilities. In most mammals the neocortex accounts for 30 percent to 40 percent of brain volume. In the highly social primates it occupies about 50 percent to 65 percent. In humans, it's 80 percent.

According to Dunbar, no such strong correlation exists between neocortex size and tasks like hunting, navigating or creating shelter. Understanding one another, it seems, is our greatest cognitive challenge. And the only way humans could handle groups of more than 50, Dunbar suggests, was to learn how to talk.

"The conventional view," Dunbar notes in his book "Grooming, Gossip and the Evolution of Language," "is that language evolved to enable males to do things like coordinate hunts more effectively. . . . I am suggesting that language evolved to allow us to gossip."

Dunbar's assertion about the origin of language is controversial. But you needn't agree with it to see that talk provides a far more powerful and efficient way to exchange social information than grooming does. In the social-brain theory's broad definition, gossip means any conversation about social relationships: who did what to whom, who is what to whom, at every level, from family to work or school group to global politics. Defined this way, gossip accounts for about two-thirds of our conversation. All this yakking — murmured asides in the kitchen, gripefests in the office coffee room — yields vital data about changing alliances; shocking machinations; new, wished-for and missed opportunities; falling kings and rising stars; dangerous rivals and potential friends. These conversations tell us too what our gossipmates think about it all, and about us, all of which is crucial to maintaining our own alliances.

For we are all gossiped about, constantly evaluated by two criteria: Whether we can contribute, and whether we can be trusted. This reflects what Ralph Adolphs, a social neuroscientist at the California Institute of Technology, calls the "complex and dynamic interplay between two opposing factors: on the one hand, groups can provide better security from predators, better mate choice and more reliable food; on the other hand, mates and food are available also to competitors from within the group." You're part of a team, but you're competing with team members. Your teammates hope you'll contribute skills and intergroup competitive spirit — without, however, offering too much competition within the group, or at least not cheating when you do. So, even if they like you, they constantly assess your trustworthiness. They know you can't afford not to compete, and they worry you might do it sneakily.

Deception runs deep. In his book, "Our Inner Ape," Frans de Waal, a primatologist at Emory University, describes a simple but cruel deception perpetrated by a female chimp named Puist. One day, Puist chases but cannot catch a younger, faster female rival. Some minutes later, writes de Waal, "Puist makes a friendly gesture from a distance, stretching out an open hand. The young female hesitates at first, then approaches Puist with classic signs of mistrust, like frequent stopping, looking around at others and a nervous grin on her face. Puist persists, adding soft pants when the younger female comes closer. Soft pants have a particularly friendly meaning; they are often followed by a kiss, the chimpanzee's chief conciliatory gesture. Then, suddenly, Puist lunges and grabs the younger female, biting her fiercely before she manages to free herself."

This "deceptive reconciliation offer," as de Waal calls it, is classic schoolyard stuff. Adult humans generally do a better job veiling a coming assault. The bigger the neocortex, the higher the rate of deceptive behavior. Our extra-big brains allow us to balance bonding and maneuvering in more subtle and complicated ways.

People with Williams, however, don't do this so well. Generating and detecting deception and veiled meaning requires not just the recognition that people can be bad but a certain level of cognitive power that people with Williams typically lack. In particular it requires what psychologists call "theory of mind," which is a clear concept of what another person is thinking and the recognition that the other person a) may see the world differently than you do and b) may actually be thinking something different from what he's saying.

Cognitive scientists argue over whether people with Williams have theory of mind. Williams people pass some theory-of-mind tests and fail others. They get many jokes, for instance, but don't understand irony. They make small talk but tend not to discuss the subtler dynamics of interpersonal relationships. Theory of mind is a slippery, multilayered concept, so the debate becomes arcane. But it's clear that Williamses do not generally sniff out the sorts of hidden meanings and intentions that lie behind so much human behavior. They would reach for Puist's outstretched hand without hesitation.

To inquire into human behavior's genetic underpinnings is to ask what most essentially defines us. One of the most vexing questions raised by both Williams research and the social-brain thesis is whether our social behavior is ultimately driven more by the urge to connect or the urge to manipulate the connection.

The traditional inclination, of course, is to distinguish essential human behavior by our "higher" skills and cognitive powers. We dominate the planet because we can think abstractly, accumulate and relay knowledge and manipulate the environment and one another. By this light our social behavior rises more from big brains than from big hearts.

Andreas Meyer-Lindenberg, a psychiatrist and neurologist, sees it differently. Meyer-Lindenberg spent the last several years at the National Institute of Mental Health exploring neural roots of mood, cognitive and behavioral disorders — including Williams syndrome, which he has investigated as part of a team led by Karen Berman, a N.I.M.H. psychiatrist, clinical neurobiologist and imaging specialist. Working with Berman and Carolyn Mervis, a developmental psychologist at the University of Louisville, Meyer-Lindenberg became convinced that we may be overvaluing the cerebral.

"Cognitive social neuroscience tends to be very top-down," Meyer-Lindenberg says. "It looks at lofty things like triadic intentionality — I'm conscious of you being conscious of me being conscious of you, things like that. Things that presuppose consciousness and elaborate intellectual procedures." The Berman group's work, however, was focused on brain networks operating, as Meyer-Lindenberg puts it, "at a lower hierarchical level."

"And the most important abnormalities in Williams," he says, "are circuits that have to do with basic regulation of emotions."

The most significant such finding is a dead connection between the orbitofrontal cortex, an area above the eye sockets and the amygdala, the brain's fear center. The orbitofrontal cortex (or OFC) is associated with (among other things) prioritizing behavior in social contexts, and earlier studies found that damage to the OFC reduces inhibitions and makes it harder to detect faux pas. The Berman team detected a new contribution to social behavior: They found that while in most people the OFC communicated with the amygdala when viewing threatening faces, the OFC in people with Williams did not. This OFC-amygdala connection worked normally, however, when people with Williams viewed nonsocial threats, like pictures of snakes, sharks or car crashes.

This appears to explain the amygdala's failure in Williams to fire at the sight of frightening faces and suggests a circuit responsible for Williamses' lack of social caution. If the results hold up, the researchers will have cleanly defined a circuit evolved specifically to warn of threats from other people. This could account not just for the lack of social fear in Williams, but with it the wariness that can motivate deeper understanding. It is possible, in short, that people with Williams miss social subtleties not just because they lack cognitive tools but because they also lack a motivation — a fear of others — that the rest of us carry to every encounter. To Meyer-Lindenberg, the primacy of such circuits suggests that human sociability rises from evolutionarily reinforced mechanisms — a raw yearning to connect; fearfulness — that are so basic they're easy to undervalue.

The disassociation of so many elements in Williams — the cognitive from the connective, social fear from nonsocial fear, the tension between the drive to affiliate and the drive to manipulate — highlights how vital these elements are and, in most of us, how delicately, critically entwined. Yet these splits in Williams also clarify which, of caring and comprehension, offers the more vital contribution. For if Williams confers disadvantage by granting more care than comprehension, reversing this imbalance creates a far more problematic phenotype.

As Robert Sapolsky of the Stanford School of Medicine puts it: "Williams have great interest but little competence. But what about a person who has competence but no warmth, desire or empathy? That's a sociopath. Sociopaths have great theory of mind. But they couldn't care less."

David Dobbs writes frequently about science and medicine. His last article for the magazine was about depression.

ADDENDUM II

The Williams Syndrome Social Phenotype: Disentangling the Contributions of Social Interest and Social Difficulties

Angela John Thurman[*,1], Marisa H. Fisher[§]

*Department of Psychiatry and Behavioral Sciences, MIND Institute, University of California, Davis, CA, USA
§Department of Counseling, Educational Psychology, and Special Education, Michigan State University, East Lansing, MI, USA
[1]Corresponding author: e-mail address: ajthurman@ucdavis.edu

Contents

Abstract

In this chapter, we provide an overview of the complex social phenotype associated with Williams syndrome (WS). We first outline the strong propensity for social interaction observed in WS, providing evidence related to the temperament, social attention, and hypersociability of individuals with WS. Second, we discuss the social cognitive difficulties, including significant weakness in interpersonal and social communication skills, observed to negatively impact reciprocal social interactions. Third, we discuss

International Review of Research in Developmental Disabilities, Volume 49
ISSN 2211-6095
http://dx.doi.org/10.1016/bs.irrdd.2015.06.002

191

the real-world implications of pairing social disinhibition with a difficulty navigating social exchanges, examining how these behaviors lead to trouble with forming and maintaining friendships, difficulties getting along with peers at school and colleagues at work, and trouble recognizing the potential dangers associated with interacting with strangers. We end with a discussion for future directions in research and practice, focusing especially on the need to move from descriptive to intervention research.

1. OVERVIEW OF WILLIAMS SYNDROME

"Friendly to the extreme" (Mendelsohn & Sancho, 2011), "what happens when you trust too much," "the opposite of autism" (Stephens, 2014), "a life without fear" (Neider, 2010), "the gregarious brain" (Dobbs, 2007)—these are just some of the descriptions used by the media to headline stories of individuals with Williams syndrome (WS). The themes depicted in these headlines are in many ways the same characteristics that captured the attention of researchers and motivated them to investigate how the behavioral features of this condition came to develop.

WS is a complex neurodevelopmental disorder caused by a deletion of ~26 genes on chromosome 7q11.23 (Hillier et al., 2003). WS is estimated to occur in 1 in 7500 live births (Strømme, Bjørnstad, & Ramstad, 2002), with both genders equally likely to be affected (American Academy of Pediatrics Committee on Genetics, 2001). There are a number of physical and medical characteristics associated with this condition including a characteristic facial appearance, congenital heart disease, connective tissue abnormalities, and growth deficiency (Morris, 2006). Early characterizations of WS described a group of individuals who presented with excellent language abilities despite the presence of severe intellectual disability. Since this period of time, there has been a growing recognition that individuals with a given syndrome, when compared to those without that syndrome, demonstrate a heightened probability of demonstrating certain behavioral outcomes, referred to as behavioral phenotypes (Dykens, 1995). This recognition has led to improvements in the methodological procedures used to characterize the specific patterns of strengths and challenges demonstrated by individuals with neurodevelopmental disorders and how these patterns change over time (e.g., Dykens & Hodapp, 1999; Fidler, Lunkenheimer, & Hahn, 2011). As a result, our current understanding of WS provides a much more nuanced characterization of the disorder.

Although there is a wide range of cognitive functioning spanning from intellectual functioning in the average range for the general population to severe intellectual disability, most children with WS present with developmental delays in early childhood and mild to moderate intellectual disability during the school-age years (e.g., Mervis & John, 2010). WS is also associated with a distinct pattern of strengths and weaknesses within the cognitive domain. Relative strengths are observed in verbal short-term memory, nonverbal reasoning, and the structural and concrete aspects of language (e.g., vocabulary); furthermore, in general, performance across these different domains is relatively comparable (Mervis & John, 2010).

In contrast, individuals with WS demonstrate a significant weakness in spatial ability, particularly visuospatial construction; with performance approximately 20 points lower than performance in the areas of nonverbal reasoning or verbal ability (e.g., Mervis et al., 2000; Mervis & John, 2010; Udwin & Yule, 1991). Because of this significant weakness in spatial ability as compared to other domains of cognitive functioning, overall IQ scores from assessments that include items assessing spatial ability often do not represent a level that fits the individual on average. This is a contributing factor to the characterization of individuals with WS as demonstrating excellent language abilities despite the presence of severe intellectual disability. It is important to note that not all individuals with WS demonstrate this specific cognitive profile, but rather, as a group there is a heightened probability of this pattern of performance relative to those who do not have WS.

Studies of the behavioral features of WS began in the 1960s (Beuren, Schultze, Eberle, Harmjanz, & Apitz, 1964; Williams, Barrett-Boys, & Lowe, 1961). Since this time, interest in WS has grown at an exponential rate. In particular, researchers have been focused on elucidating how the unique social profile associated with this condition comes to develop. Individuals with WS demonstrate extreme interest in interacting with other people (Klein-Tasman, Li-Barber, & Magargee, 2011; Klein-Tasman & Mervis, 2003; Mervis et al., 2003). Descriptions such as gregarious and overly friendly (Gosch & Pankau, 1997), charming (Fryns, Borghgraef, Volcke, & Van den Berge, 1991), and never going unnoticed in a group (Dykens & Rosner, 1999) are frequently used within the literature to describe individuals with WS. These behavioral characteristics are likely the driving factor behind the portrayal of WS as the opposite of autism spectrum disorder (ASD) (e.g., Cowley, 2003; Levy et al., 2011).

Despite their sociable nature, however, there are a number of difficulties demonstrated by individuals with WS when it comes to navigating the world of people around them. Individuals with WS are frequently reported to have considerable difficulty establishing and maintaining peer relationships (e.g., Davies, Udwin, & Howlin, 1998; Sullivan, Winner, & Tager-Flusberg,

2003) and evidence suggests that, as adults, most individuals with WS are isolated and seldom engage in social interactions with peers (Davies et al., 1998; Rosner, Hodapp, Fidler, Sagun, & Dykens, 2004; Udwin, 1990). This seemingly paradoxical combination of relatively good language abilities, an extremely sociable and friendly disposition, and significant difficulty with reciprocal—social interactions has intrigued both researchers and the public alike.

In this chapter, we provide an overview of the complex social phenotype associated with WS. We outline what we know today about the strong propensity for social interaction observed in WS, the social cognitive difficulties observed to negatively impact reciprocal social interactions, and the real-world implications of pairing social disinhibition with a difficulty navigating social exchanges. We end with a discussion for future directions in research and practice, focusing especially on the need to move from descriptive to intervention research.

Printed in the United States
By Bookmasters